God's Thoughts and Ways are Above Ours

Especially in the Forgiveness of Sins

In several sermons on Isaiah 55:7–9:

"Let the wicked forsake his way, and the unrighteous man his thoughts: and let him return unto the LORD, and He will have mercy upon him; and to our God, for He will abundantly pardon. 'For My thoughts are not your thoughts, neither are your ways My ways,' saith the LORD. 'For as the heavens are higher than the earth, so are My ways higher than your ways, and My thoughts than your thoughts.' "

By John Shower
Pastor of Currier's Hall, London

Edited by Dr. Don Kistler

Soli Deo Gloria Publications
. . . for instruction in righteousness. . .

Soli Deo Gloria Publications
A division of Soli Deo Gloria Ministries, Inc.
P. O. Box 451, Morgan, PA 15064
(412) 221-1901/Fax (412) 221-1902
www.SDGbooks.com

*

*

ISBN 1-57358-149-6

Library of Congress Cataloging-in-Publication Data

Shower, John, 1657-1715.
  God's thoughts and ways are above ours, especially in the forgiveness of sins / by John Shower; edited by Don Kistler.
    p. cm.
  ISBN 1-57358-149-6
  1. Forgiveness of sin. I. Kistler, Don. II. Title.
BT795 .S48 2003
252–dc21
                                        2003009913

Contents

Preface

I am encouraged to think that the following sermons did good when they were preached, and, with the hope that they may be of some further use, they are now published. It has been desired that I would transcribe them in the words wherein they were delivered, which, with very little variation, I have consented to. It may be that the peculiar turn of expression, though popular and less exact in the pulpit, which renders the plain truths of Christianity acceptable to most hearers, may be more useful and more affecting to several readers than what is more concise, and in more studied expressions.

I can never reckon it a fault in a sermon that the style is different from what is expected in a close and just discourse, or that what might be said in two words or sentences is expressed in three or four. Perhaps the greatest part of the hearers need such enlargement and repetition, and their capacity could not otherwise be reached so as to profit them any more than that game may be taken by an unspread net.

Very wise men have thought that it is a mistake in a conscientious preacher to endeavor to please only a few of the more knowing and judicious hearers. But that which is suited to do good to the generality of those we preach to will ordinarily be best thought of by wise men, whose capacity and judgment could reach what was more accurate. For they must know that it would not be proper here; they themselves have sins to be forgiven, corruptions to be mortified, and immortal souls to be saved—and so do their inferiors. And there is but one way for the learned and unlearned to get to heaven that I know of.

It is true that the things treated will be despised by many who do not relish what is contained in such discourses. The matter is out of their way. They are not sensible of sin, nor solicitous about forgiveness, and so do not think themselves concerned. It is to be feared that there are many others who hear and read sermons only to judge them, without any desire of advantage to their souls. They are not better for the sermons they commend any more than by those they condemn. They may say, perhaps, "It was an excellent discourse; he's a good orator and a judicious preacher, and this sermon exceeded even his last one," but their consciences are not touched, and they feel nothing that does them any real good.

However, there are multitudes in this city and nation who will be thankful for any such assistance to prevent their despair when convinced of sin; as the doctrine of God's free grace in forgiveness that is displayed in the first four sermons. And others, who meet with objections in conversation, and in pamphlets against the Christian doctrine of the sacred Trinity, the incarnation of Christ, and God's wise government of the world from the unaccountable passages of providence (which are apt to cause them to stumble), may be willing to consider and improve this argument of God's thoughts not being as ours, but far above our reach, which is the subject of the fifth sermon.

Let me only add that many younger ministers, as well as elder ones, have died of late. And though few of us will be missed when we die (there being such numbers to supply our places), yet everyone should endeavor to be as useful as he can while he lives, for the night is hastening wherein no work can be done. If any reader gets good, let him give God the glory. I most earnestly beg His blessing to that end.

John Shower

1

The Text Opened

"Let the wicked forsake his way, and the unrighteous man his thoughts, and let him return unto the Lord, and He will have mercy upon him; and to our God, for He will abundantly pardon. 'For My thoughts are not your thoughts, neither are your ways My ways,' saith the Lord. 'For as the heavens are higher than the earth, so are My ways higher than your ways, and My thoughts than your thoughts.' " Isaiah 55:7–9

There are three things to be considered in this passage:

There is a call to repentance, by a double precept or injunction of duty. The persons concerned in it are set forth under two names, to take in all sorts of sinners: the wicked and the unrighteous. And the duty is doubly expressed: to forsake their evil ways and thoughts, and to return to the Lord. These are the two parts of true repentance: turning from sin and returning to God.

There is an encouraging promise, that God will have mercy on such penitents and will abundantly pardon them. He will interest them in the sure mercies of David (verse 3), or in all the blessings of the everlasting covenant by Christ. It is of Him you must understand, (verse 4–6), of whom David was only a type: "Behold I have given him for a witness to the people, a leader and commander to the people."

There is the ground and reason why we may believe this promise shall be made good: "For My thoughts are not as your thoughts, saith the Lord God, but as high as the heavens are above the earth. . . ." That is to say "There is a vast disparity between My thoughts and yours; and Mine are transcendently above yours, as far as heaven is above the earth. And so are My ways above your ways." This is true as to God's thoughts and purposes of grace in pardoning sinners, and as to the effects of those kind purposes in His ways and works. And the highest assurance of the truth of all this is added from a divine testimony annexed: "Thus saith the Lord." He who best knows His own gracious designs has told us this; and by our believing it we set our seals to it that God is true.

Several things might be observed as being proper to be discoursed of from these words:

First, if ever sinners find mercy with God, they must forsake their former evil ways and course of life.

Second, it is not enough for such to reform their outward practice and forsake their evil ways, but they must be changed and sanctified in heart; their evil thoughts must be forsaken.

Third, it is not sufficient to turn from sin and wickedness in heart and life without returning unto God.

Fourth, the worst of sinners, be they wicked as to sins against God, or unrighteous as to iniquity against men, yet if they turn from their evil ways and return to the Lord, they shall find mercy. Though you have sinned (as you might think) so as never any did before, condemn yourselves as the chief of sinners, and have refused the pardoning mercy of God formerly offered, all this may be forgiven. And it is implied that it shall be forgiven upon every new invitation and call to repentance, so that where sin has abounded, grace shall much more abound.

Fifth, He will have mercy and will abundantly pardon; let a man consider the certainty of this and thereupon return. We may here observe that the great motive and encouragement which puts sinners on forsaking their evil ways and turning to God is a sensible apprehension that there is mercy and forgiveness to be had. There could be no repentance without it; nor would it be required of us as a duty, to repent and return, if there were no forgiveness with God.

Sixth, besides the general encouragement of finding mercy with God, there is the special kind of mercy which the sinner needs, and that is pardon. I may here observe that pardoning mercy to returning sinners is mercy indeed; it is, of all others, the most suitable and most welcome.

Seventh, God will not only show mercy to returning sinners, but He will abundantly pardon them. He will multiply pardons.

Let us now examine each of these points.

1. If ever sinners find mercy with God, they must forsake their evil ways. The ordinary course of any man's life is very fitly called his way, that which is his ordinary practice, his daily walk. Accordingly we read of the way of a sinner, the path of the wicked, and the way of evil men. This is often called our own way, in opposition to the way of truth and righteousness, which is called the way of the Lord, or God's way, because He directs and approves it, enables us to walk in it, and rewards us for

so doing.

This is the great difference between the righteous and the wicked. Their course and way are different. A good man may make a false step; he may stumble or step out of the way in a particular instance, but he does not work iniquity. He does not walk in the way of the ungodly; his course and conversation mainly is otherwise. And 'tis not for one or two particular actions, good or bad, that a man is to be denominated a good or wicked man, but from his ordinary course of life. If that is wicked, he must forsake it, or never find mercy with God. And this must be done heartily and unfeignedly, speedily and without delay, impartially and universally, with full purpose of heart to persevere and never again return to folly. Without this, there can be no converse with God, nor communion with Him. "Wash ye, make ye clean, put away the evil of your doings, then come and let us reason together" (Isaiah 1:16, 18).

Till this is resolved upon and begun, you are impenitent, and so are abominable in the sight of God. For certainly God will not dishonor His perfections, contradict His Word, and prostitute His grace to justify the ungodly while they continue as such, without desiring, resolving, and endeavoring to forsake their evil ways. Wherever Christ is a Savior, to give remission of sin, He also gives them repentance (Acts 5:31).

2. It is not enough for one who expects to find mercy with God to reform his practices and forsake his evil ways, but he must be inwardly sanctified, his heart renewed, and his very thoughts changed. "Let the wicked forsake his way, and the unrighteous man his thoughts. . . ." His thoughts, especially his false, unjust, unrighteous thoughts of God, must be forsaken,

whereof sinners have very many. Here the change must be, because the heart is the principal seat of sin or grace, of sincerity or hypocrisy. It is in the inward thoughts and affections of the heart that sanctification or carnality principally discloses itself. Till the fountain is cleansed, the streams will be polluted. The unsanctified heart is the source of evil thoughts, words, and actions. "Wash thy heart, O Jerusalem! How long shall vain thoughts lodge in thee?" (Jeremiah 4:14). "As a man thinketh in his heart, so is he" (Proverbs 23:7). The thoughts of the wicked, or wicked thoughts, are an abomination in the sight of God (Proverbs 15:26). And 'tis the design of the gospel, and the glory of it, beyond all the philosophy in the world, to bring our thoughts into obedience to Christ. While any wickedness is indulged, and allowed in the heart and thoughts, no outward reformation (as to our behavior before the world), no abstinence from gross pollutions and disorders in the life, will denominate us as truly penitent or give us hopes of finding mercy with God while we regard iniquity in our hearts, while the heart goes after covetousness, filthiness, or any allowed lust. Unless the thoughts are changed as well as the outward course, unless the heart is sanctified as well as the conversation reformed, there is no forgiveness. You know the woe which our Savior denounced against the Pharisees on this account (Matthew 23:25), whom He characterized as hypocrites because they cleaned the outside of the cup and platter, but within were full of extortion and excess. Like whited sepulchers they appeared beautiful outwardly, but were within full of dead men's bones and all uncleanness.

3. Observe further that 'tis not enough to turn from

sin and wickedness in heart and life, but if you would find mercy with God you must return to the Lord. To clear this, consider that we have departed and gone off from God by sin, both as our Chief Good and Sovereign Lord. We have abandoned and forsaken Him as our portion and felicity, and as our Lord and Ruler. It is necessary, therefore, that we return to Him so as to value His favor as our very life, place all our happiness in His love and likeness, observe His orders, and endeavor to please Him. We must seek His honor, make it our business to glorify Him, and be entirely devoted to Him as our Ultimate End. Without resolving on this, there's no ground to expect mercy in the pardon of the least sin; and upon this we may hope for forgiveness of the greatest.

Men may break off a course of notorious, open wickedness upon various and different motives, and then take up with a negative religion without returning to God. They may satisfy themselves that now they don't commit the same crimes as before; they may think it enough that they are not as bad as others are, or as they once were themselves. But this is not sufficient if they are destitute of love for God, if they are not careful to please Him, if His glory is not their end, if they do not eye His authority, if they are not chiefly concerned to be accepted by Him, if they do not choose Him as the Portion of their soul, and by an entire resignation of themselves make Him Lord of all; to govern their actions by the counsels of His Word, and to dispose and order their conditions by His most wise and holy providence. Such a turning to the Lord must be joined with a forsaking of sin.

4. Let the wicked and unrighteous man forsake the

evil of his heart and ways and turn to the Lord, and he shall find mercy. I observe that if the vilest and most heinous transgressors (let their sins be what they will) penitently return to God, they may be assured of pardon. Whatever wickedness against God or unrighteousness against men, whatever iniquity or sin in heart or life, open or secret, they are charged with, yet there is mercy with God upon true repentance. The Holy Scriptures are full of this doctrine. How large and general are the invitations and calls of God to all sorts of sinners? How express and positive are the declarations of His Word? He says that even scarlet and crimson sins shall be as snow and wool; that all sin and blasphemy shall be forgiven except that against the Holy Ghost, which is joined with obstinate impenitence; that our Lord Jesus Christ came to save the chief of sinners, and that His blood cleanses from all sin. What a large and black catalogue is there of such as shall not enter into the kingdom of God—fornicators, adulterers, idolaters, sodomites, drunkards, revilers, and extortioners—and yet 'tis added, "Such were some of you, but ye are washed" (1 Corinthians 6:9–11). He is a God who pardons iniquity, transgression, and sin (Micah 7:18). How affectionately God expostulates with sinners, even the vilest of them, and urges them to cast away their transgressions, and then assures them that He has no pleasure in their ruin? How earnestly He beseeches them to be reconciled, and to hearken to the voice of His mercy! With what a variety of arguments He pleads with them from the greatness of His mercy offered, from the freeness and riches of His grace, from the absolute necessity of it, and from the hazard they run of being undone forever if they refuse it! What instances are there of the blackest crimes forgiven, and the most heinous offenders received to favor, with the assurance that others may be so too if they will return? "Cease to do evil, learn to do well. Come now and let us reason together" (Isaiah 1:16–18), that is, nothing passed shall be a bar to your reconciliation if you will now return; no sin that you have ever committed shall be your undoing if you will now accept mercy.

I say this to every man and woman in this assembly, and should there be any who think that they have sinned with such peculiar aggravations as never any did who were forgiven (which I believe is untrue), yet suppose it true, the free grace and mercy of God has never yet been tried to the utmost. It can outdo all it has ever done. The aggravations of your guilt can never be such as to condemn you, but the virtue of the blood of Christ is greater to pardon you if you return to God by Jesus Christ. As far as heaven is above earth, God's thoughts are above ours in this matter.

There is an instance in the beginning of the Bible as to how different God's thoughts are from ours, and how much above them they are. "I will not curse the ground any more for man's sake," God says in Genesis 8, "because the imagination of the heart of man is only evil, and continually evil." One would rather think that God, for that reason, would do nothing but curse it; but it seems to intimate, as if the kind thoughts of God were to this purpose: "If I should never leave cursing till man leaves sinning, I would do nothing but curse; but I will not do that."

"I can't hope to find mercy; my sin is so great," says a convinced sinner, not considering that 'tis the glory of God to forgive a multitude of sins, and that where sin has abounded, there is an opportunity for grace much more to abound. The psalmist uses it as an argument in prayer: "Lord, forgive mine iniquity, for it is great" (Psalm 25:11). This is an argument fit to be used nowhere else. The greatness of his sin made him fly to God for pardon, but did not keep him from returning. This is the scope and tenor of the whole gospel: "To this do all the prophets and apostles witness, that through the name of Christ, whoever believes on Him (without distinction) shall receive the forgiveness of sin." If you are weary and heavy laden, sensible of sin and desirous to forsake it; if you see your need of Christ, and flee to the refuge of hope set before you, you may, you ought to believe that you shall find mercy, rest and forgiveness.

To encourage the worst of sinners to repent, it is observed in all ages that many wicked people who find mercy with God and are forgiven have been much more vile than several of those who are left to perish in their sins and shall never be forgiven. How many who have been kept from gross pollutions and made a longer and fairer profession of religion than others, who have abounded in outward duties, who have been of more useful parts, endowments, and qualifications, more considerable for their wit, learning, and other accomplishments (more capable, one would think, of doing service in the world and the church, and for the glory of God, if converted)—how many such are yet left to perish in their impenitence and unbelief, while others have been called, and have been turned, justified, sanctified and saved, who have labored under many contrary discouragements and disadvantages, especially by the heinousness of their former guilt and rebellion.

Therefore consider it seriously: if you have been a great sinner, God is a gracious God, and Christ is a mighty Savior, able to save to the uttermost all who come to God by Him. He can as easily forgive five hundred talents as fifty pence. Though the debtors are very different in the parable (Luke 7:41), He frankly forgave them both. Not only such as have sinned in some lesser degrees may hope to find mercy, but they who have run out into the grossest wickedness, impiety, unrighteousness, and iniquity; not only such as have neglected one, two, or ten calls to repentance by the gospel, but if they have done so for many years to this very hour, they may yet find mercy if they forsake their evil ways and return to God by Jesus Christ.

Let your sins past be what they will, say as bad as you will or can of yourselves, and of the dreadful aggravations of your guilt; clothe it with all the horror and darkness possible, yet, as high as the heavens are above the earth, so is the mercy of God, and the merit and virtue of the blood of Christ above your guilt.

OBECTION. But I have stood out for so long, persisted in my wickedness for so many years, stifled the motions of God's Spirit so often, and been deaf to the voice of God's Word and my own conscience, that I fear He will never accept me, nor ever show mercy to me. For He called and I would not come. He knocked and I would not open. And therefore, if I call, I may expect to find the door shut.

ANSWER. As long as His Word abides faithful, the covenant of grace is everlasting and unrepealed, and the offers of God's grace are repeated; as long as there's a new proclamation of mercy made in the name of Christ, though all the former have been despised, you may come in, find mercy, and be accepted. For every new offer of God's grace carries in it the offer and promise of the pardon of all your former refusals, if you will now consent. The promise is as free, and the performance of it as sure, now as ever. You may come in now and be pardoned and saved upon as free and gracious terms as several years ago. 'Tis still without money and without price. Your long unbelief and obstinacy does not raise the price nor alter the terms. Therefore, plead the riches of His free grace, and do it the more thankfully and humbly, the more vile you have been. Say, "Lord, Thy mercy will be the more honored, Thy free grace will be the more magnified and exalted in the conversion and forgiveness of such a wretch, in the purging such a defiled soul, in the healing such a leper, in the pardoning so many and great transgressions."

And 'tis often observed that when such sinners return to God, they have the advantage of others on several accounts, wherein God is more glorified by them. Usually they admire the grace of God more than others, love God and Christ more, walk more humbly with God, are more charitable, tender, and compassionate to other Christians, and are usually more watchful and circumspect for the time to come, more afraid of falling. Commonly they are more abundant in service for the honor of God, more entirely devoted to Him, more zealous for His glory, more of a public spirit, and are more ready to do and to suffer anything for His sake. As this tends to the honor of God, so it may be pleaded in prayer.

OBJECTION. There's no finding mercy and forgiveness with God without faith in Jesus Christ, and I can't believe in my heart that Christ will receive me. I cannot persuade myself that such a one as I should be accepted. Shall the invaluable purchase of the death of Christ belong to me, be bestowed on me? If you gave me all the world, I can't believe that such a wretch as I have been shall find mercy. You don't know how I have affronted, dishonored, despised, and disobeyed Him. I have abused His grace at such a dreadful rate that you can't imagine the aggravation of my sins or the sadness of my case. I can't believe that He will ever forgive me, receive me, justify me, and glorify me. I can't believe it, and if I can't believe in Christ I can't be saved by Him."

ANSWER. Don't mistake the nature of saving faith. You say that you can't believe and have no faith. But you mean no more than that as yet you are not certain of salvation; you have no assurance. But are you willing to receive Christ Jesus as offered in the gospel? Has the Spirit of God so far convinced you of your sinful, miserable state that you heartily consent to be saved by Christ in His own way and upon His own terms? Are you willing to take Him as your Teacher, Savior, and Lord? Are you brought to depend and trust entirely upon the mercy of God in Jesus Christ as the only Mediator between God and man? Are you willing to rely upon His sacrifice and meritorious righteousness as your only refuge and hope? Do you desire to be found in Him alone, to be accepted by God only in the Beloved? Are you truly willing and, as far as you know your own hearts, are you resolved to follow Him as the Captain of your salvation wherever He shall lead you in hope of His purchased and promised grace and glory? This is faith, and dare you say that there's nothing of this that appears in the temper of your spirits?

If you can't with any confidence say this, yet the case is hopeful if you are in the number of convinced, awakened, sensible sinners. Are you sensible of your ignorance, poverty, guilt, impurity, bondage, and unrighteousness, and that you need Christ as a complete Savior, to be made of God unto us wisdom, righteousness, sanctification, and redemption; to expiate sin by His blood, and to subdue it by His Spirit; to reconcile us to God, and begin that blessed union and communion here which shall be complete in heaven? This comprehends our whole salvation. Christ is the Savior of sinners, of such as are lost, who apprehend themselves to be so without His help, who feel their sins and their wants. He did not come to call the righteous, but sinners to repentance. He is a Physician not to the whole, but to the sick. He calls and cures not the proud, but the humble; not the full, but the hungry; not the rich, but the poor; not the free, but the captives who are sensible of their bonds; not the righteous, but sinners. And He makes you, by His Spirit, thus humble, empty, hungry, and sensible of sin so that you may look to Him as the great Reconciler, sensible of the need of pardon.

If it is thus, you may then look for redemption through the blood of Jesus, even the forgiveness of sins. Feeling your need of sanctification, you may look to be washed, cleansed, and sanctified in the name of the Lord Jesus, and by His Spirit. Feeling your want of strength to do and suffer the will of God, you may look to Christ to enable you to do all things. Now one who is not fully satisfied and assured that Christ will save him may yet be brought to this frame. How is it with you as to this?

Further, under the sense of being vile and heinous sinners, are you brought earnestly to desire the mercy of God in Christ, and diligently to seek after Him? Though you sometimes fear that He will not accept you, yet do you not neglect to pray to Him? What would you not give that you might be interested in God's pardoning mercy and accepted in Christ? Are not your greatest fears and concerns with respect to this that He would reject you? Are not the strongest desires of your souls that He would receive you? And is it thus not only at a pinch, in affliction and trouble as to outward affairs, or on a sickbed, but in health and prosperity? Is this the language of your souls: "I have health, friends, money, credit, and many outward blessings beyond others. I lack nothing for my body, or for my comfortable passage through this world, but I am yet a miserable creature if I am under the guilt of sin, if God is not reconciled to me. Oh, that I were clear as to this! What I would give to be at peace with God, and to have an encouraging sense of it!"

Are you sensible of your past unkindness to this merciful God and gracious Savior so as to bewail it? Is it now the ground of your fear and trouble, not only that you have sinned against the light of nature (though, it may be, you were first awakened by the sense of some such transgression), but now you are troubled for the contempt of the gospel, for your neglect of Christ, the Savior of sinners, for refusing Him when He has called and invited you? And are ready to say within yourselves, "Oh, with what earnestness did He call me to accept His mercy! How freely He offered to forgive me! He would have been my Savior, but I would not receive Him. With what folly and obstinacy I hardened my heart, stopped my ears, and turned my back on Him? I resisted Him in both His Word and Spirit." Does this grieve and trouble you, as well as the gross pollutions of the world, which natural light will condemn?

Your case is hopeful, notwithstanding the sense of your vileness and fears on that account, if you yet resolve to follow on in seeking mercy and forgiveness of God by Jesus Christ 'till you obtain it. Do you resolve you will wait, pray, wrestle, and persevere therein till it shall please God to cast an eye of pity and compassion on your miserable souls? Will you continue in the use of God's appointed means, where He communicates His Spirit and conveys grace, and where He is wont to vouchsafe His presence? Will you inquire of everybody who may assist you as to how you may be one of those happy souls whom God will abundantly pardon? Can you say this, "Though I fear and doubt, yet I seek and strive, and will not give up. I will not desist, I will not depart from His door. I am undone if He refuses me; and if I perish and die in my sins, and am damned for them, it shall be in seeking mercy and begging mercy for Christ's sake." And if you can say this truly, you may be assured that you shall not perish, but shall find mercy.

Can you say this, and is it the real language of your heart? Nothing in all the Word shall content and satisfy you, nor is it ever likely to do so, till you have some good hope through grace of finding mercy with God. You search the Scriptures, search your hearts, go to ministers, consult friends, and attend ordinances with this desire and design; and you pray before you come to hear that some seasonable, powerful word may drop and reach your case. "Alas, I used to hear formerly after another manner and with other thoughts. I judged the minister, passing sentence on the sermon, or considering only how it concerned others. But now I apply all to myself; now I look for my own portion and watch for that which principally concerns me. And, by the grace of God, I will thus attend and wait and watch at the posts of wisdom's door that I may find life (Proverbs 8:34). Though I have but very little hope, and a great many fears, considering what a vile sinner I have been, yet I do not utterly despair. I am told that I must not despair, and that despair is a sin and hope a duty. Therefore I will yet hold on, wait upon the Lord, and seek His mercy: Though I can't pray with confidence, I will yet look up; though I can't say I believe, yet I'll not utterly despair; though I have sinned against the grace of the gospel and the blood and Spirit of Christ, yet I hope, not above and beyond the help and benefit of His grace, gospel, blood, and Spirit. I'll therefore hold on and wait in hope in the diligent use of all the means of salvation."

5. I proceed to another thing observable from these words: "Let him return, and He will have mercy, and abundantly pardon." Let him think of that and return; believe that and be encouraged to return. I observe that the great motive and encouragement to put a sinner about forsaking his evil ways and returning to God is the sensible apprehension that there's mercy to be had; that God will forgive and abundantly pardon the penitent, returning sinner. I confess, 'tis not an easy matter to be persuaded of the doctrine of the forgiveness of sin. Whatever guess and conjecture men may have about it, from the divine patience and forbearance to a sinful world in the continuance of His forfeited mercy,

yet (see Nathanael Taylor's *Preservative Against Deism*) without the gospel revelation we can have no certainty about this. The Gentiles had some imaginations and hopes that their gods were placable and inclined to pardon, and that was the rise of their expiations and sacrifices; but they had no assured promise or covenant to build upon. They did not know the Mediator between God and man by His own sacrifice of Himself to make atonement. 'Tis the language of the law written on our hearts, that "the soul that sinneth shall die." It is the voice of natural conscience that guilt and punishment are inseparable. And were there not something known of the doctrine of forgiveness by the revelation of it which God has made, this would be the common sentiment of mankind.

I need not consider what particular ways and methods God may have to reveal this pardoning mercy unto any who are strangers to the written Word, or whether He has done so. It does not belong to us to be curious in inquiring about other men who shall be judged by a righteous God, according to the law they were under and the light they had. 'Tis certain that even among those to whom the gospel is preached, whoever they are who are deeply convinced of sin and have had their conscience awakened to apprehend the holiness and justice of God, 'tis one of the most difficult things in the world to persuade them that God will have mercy and abundantly pardon. It is one great Work of the Holy Spirit to satisfy the soul of this. There's no serious minister of Christ who has not had abundant experience of this in those who are awakened to any concern for their soul's salvation. There is sufficient evidence of this in David's case in Psalm 130:3–4: "If thou, Lord, shouldst mark iniquities, O Lord, who should stand? But there is forgiveness with Thee." If God should mark sin so as to proceed to punish it according to His righteous law, who could stand? Who would escape condemnation? Or, when accused, who could stand in the judgment so as to be acquitted? 'Tis not my own case alone that, if God should be strict and severe with me, I am an undone and lost creature. But 'tis true of all the world. The holiest saint on earth can't be justified in His sight; and what then would become of me, who has such a load of guilt, and so many heinous crimes to acknowledge? In this sense we find the expression of "standing" used. Romans 14:4: "To his own Master he standeth or falleth," that is, shall either be acquitted or condemned by God. 'Tis of the same import as Psalm 143:2: "Enter not into judgment with Thy Servant, O Lord, for in Thy sight no flesh living shall be justified."

Consider a little with what a frame of spirit David uses such language. He seems to cry out in the view of his heinous sins as ready to despair if not relieved by the hope that there is forgiveness with God. "Lord, who can stand?" That is, how justly may I be condemned if I am tried at Thy bar? According to strict justice, I must be cast. I cannot answer Thee for one abomination, much less for all of mine. I cannot stand in the judgment. This will be, and is, the case of all convinced sinners, of everyone of us when we view our sins, and the Majesty of heaven whom we have offended; when we consider how we have affronted and despised God, how easily He can crush us into hell, and how justly He might; when we think how we have preferred a lust, a trifle, a passion, a humor before Him; how we have slighted His authority, abused His goodness, defied His power, wearied His patience, rejected His grace, and, by numberless, aggravated transgressions, incurred the vengeance He has threatened, and made ourselves liable to His intolerable and everlasting wrath. Under such a sight and sense of sin, what can relieve but the consideration that there's mercy and forgiveness with God, and that He'll abundantly pardon returning sinners?

This, I say, we are backward to believe. There's so much ignorance and blindness in the minds of sinners; there's such a proneness in men to judge God by themselves, and of His thoughts and ways by their own. They think that, because they could not pardon such and such heinous provocations so often repeated, God will not. And there are so many fears and jealousies in our guilty souls concerning God that, without the encouragement of such a declaration of grace as we have in this text, there could be no repentance; there would be no returning to God. You know what Benhadad's servants told him in 1 Kings 20:31: "We have heard that the kings of Israel are merciful kings; let us put sackcloth on our loins and ropes about our necks, and go to the King of Israel; peradventure he will save thy life." This gracious method God used toward Israel in Jeremiah 3:12: "Go, and proclaim these words toward the north, saying, 'Return, O backsliding Israel,' saith the Lord, 'and I will not cause My anger to fall upon you; for I am merciful,' saith the Lord, 'and will not keep anger forever.' " Only acknowledge the iniquity that you have transgressed against the Lord your God, that is, "Let them not cherish any such hard thoughts of Me, as if there were no forgiveness; let them not despair of My mercy, as if I would not receive them when they return."

This gives the greatest encouragement to sinners that here is a plank to save them from shipwreck, a remedy against despair. Here's a ground for them to return to God with hopes. Here's a motive to seek mercy, that God has proclaimed His readiness to forgive and His abundant pardon. I think that it is very plain that the doctrine of repentance would never have been preached if there were no hope of forgiveness. The fallen angels, having no mercy offered, were never called to repent; for let there be never so deep conviction of sin and sorrow for it, there could be no repenting and returning to God without believing that mercy might be had. All would end in death and desperation. Repentance would never be commanded as a duty (it could not, if we believe the wisdom, goodness, and faithfulness of God) were it not for this truth, that if the wicked forsakes his way and returns to God he will find pardon. But upon the consideration of this, sinners begin to have good thoughts of God. Many of their scruples are removed; many of their objections are answered, and they are now encouraged to seek the mercy of God and prepare themselves to receive it.

To conclude, therefore, let the vilest and worst of sinners receive these glad tidings of God's grace and not abuse them. Don't despise this message; don't neglect it, but consider how much you need this mercy. Then go home and earnestly beg for it. Endeavor to welcome it as it is offered in the gospel; and then plead it, and urge it for Christ's sake according to the promise, since it is free mercy. Stir up your souls to hope in it, knowing that God takes pleasure in those who hope in His mercy.

May I not therefore say that 'tis from the devil (for whom there is no mercy), if there are any of you to whom this doctrine is preached who will yet conclude that there is no mercy for you? Since God has told us that if the wicked forsakes his evil ways and thoughts, and turns to the Lord, they may and ought in that case most firmly believe that He will have mercy, and that He will abundantly pardon.

2

Pardoning Mercy Is the Most Valuable Mercy

"Let the wicked forsake his way, and the unrighteous man his thoughts, and let him return unto the Lord, and He will have mercy upon him; and to our God, for He will abundantly pardon." Isaiah 55:7

It is of the sixth observation from these words that I would now speak (without repeating the other five), that pardoning mercy to penitent sinners is mercy indeed, the most valuable and seasonable mercy. This I shall endeavor to manifest by several considerations, and then apply it.

First, there's nothing more suitable to the case of a guilty sinner who has any thoughts of returning to God. Consider the perplexities of one who is awakened to a sense of sin, and is under a spirit of conviction. His bitter complaints and loud cries tell us that he does not know what to do, nor how to be rid of his burden. He apprehends his danger from unpardoned sin, and feels the lack of this forgiveness; he is wounded, and nothing but the voice of pardoning mercy can heal him. "I have greatly sinned," said David, and his heart smote him. "And now, I beseech thee, O Lord, take away the iniquity of Thy servant" (2 Samuel 24:10). Nothing else could give him ease and quiet from an accusing, troubled conscience. "The inhabitant shall not say, 'I am sick'; the people that dwell therein shall be forgiven their iniquity" (Isaiah 33:24). The mere patience and forbearance of God, without forgiveness, will not answer the exigence of his case. Though he is yet out of hell, he does not know how long it shall be so, or how soon he may there have a miserable portion. It is the sense of unpardoned sin that breaks his bones, dries up his marrow, and sticks like an arrow in his flesh— whereas pardoning mercy is as health to the navel, marrow to the bones, and a cordial to his heart, yea, even as life from the dead. And dead he is in law, as if under a sentence of condemnation, till he is interested in forgiveness by faith in the blood of Jesus. Then may he lift up his head, as one alive from the dead, and admit consolation, when he can hope his sins are forgiven and that God is reconciled. "Comfort ye, comfort ye My people. Say unto Jerusalem, 'Her warfare is accomplished; her iniquity is forgiven' " (Isaiah 40:1–2). "Blessed is the man whose iniquity is forgiven, and sin covered" (Psalm 32:1). Till then, they are under the curse of God, a curse that cuts them off from God, and all gracious communications from Him; a curse which pierces deep, spreads far, and makes the whole creation at enmity with us. This curse is intolerable in its effects, and unavoidable too. There is no relief or remedy against it but by the New Covenant, and faith in Jesus Christ. 'Tis only by the redemption we have in Jesus Christ through His blood, even the forgiveness of sins, in which forgiveness we can never be interested without repentance towards God and faith in our Lord Jesus Christ. "There is no rest in my bones because of my sin," said the psalmist in Psalm 38:3. "My sins are a heavy burden; they are too heavy for me" (verse 4). Till this burden is removed by forgiveness, what ease or rest can a sinner enjoy?

It is true, the deceit of sensual pleasures, or the hurry and clatter of worldly business, may hinder the sense of this for a while and keep all quiet. Yet sooner or later, the sinful soul will have torment: Conscience will awaken. Men may laugh and be merry for a time; they may try to be confident and secure under the wrath and curse of God; they may take their poison for their antidote, their wound for their plaster, their plague for their cure, their disease for their remedy, and so may try to preserve a little false peace—but the end will be the most horrid despair. And the more jovial and airy, careless and presumptuous they have been in health and prosperity, under the guilt of great transgressions, the more disconsolate will such be when conscience awakens to set their sins in order before them.

Is there then any message like that of forgiveness that will suit the case of such? They can relish nothing else, and can think of nothing else. This is what they aim at. The subject of their great inquiry is how they may be forgiven. They may try in vain to see what company, mirth, sports, business, or superstition will do. They must come to God for pardon or they cannot find rest. Hosea 5:13: "When Ephrahim saw his sickness, and Judah saw his wound, then went Ephraim to the Assyrian, and sent to King Jareb; yet could he not heal you, nor cure you of your wound."

Do you know the misery and danger of a sinful soul, unreconciled to God, bound over to His eternal wrath, every moment exposed as a guilty wretch to His fiery vengeance? Do you consider the case of such a one, who has all the plagues and curses in the Book of God in force against him, and nothing but a little breath between him and endless ruin; who can't tell but that the next day or minute death may open the door and let him fall into damnation? Does anyone rightly understand this, believe it, consider it, and apply it as his own case? What mercy will suit such a one but pardoning mercy? What is all the pomp and glory of this world to such a man without the forgiveness of sin? How can he eat, drink, sleep, or trade, or do anything, without some hope of pardon, without seeking it, without endeavoring it, without using means in order to accomplish it?

Second, pardoning mercy is mercy indeed, as it is the fruit of covenant love, an effect of the special, distinguishing love of God: This is the great priviledge of such whose God is the Lord. This is a covenant blessing that's never given in anger. This is never bestowed but as a favor that is peculiar to God's people. This is always accompanied with regeneration and adoption. As Scripture says, "I will be their God, and will forgive their iniquity. Happy is the man whose iniquity is forgiven. Happy is the people whose God is the Lord."

Third, this mercy is the most comprehensive blessing, and the foundation of many other mercies. This mercy secures our state, sweetens our other blessings, lays the foundation for peace of conscience, gives freedom of access to the throne of grace, and makes way for communion with God in all ordinances: This clears us from the accusation of Satan, the condemnation of the law, and the condemnation of our own hearts; for who shall lay anything to his charge whom God forgives? We can have no right and title to eternal life without this; for the legal bar must be removed by the pardon of sin as well as the moral incapacity by the sanctifying

Spirit. The great blessings of the gospel—such as the spirit of holiness, communion with God, and so on— are promised to accompany this one of forgiveness. Hebrews 8:12: "I will be merciful to their unrighteousness, and their iniquities I will remember no more." By this we not only escape the punishment due to sin, which would render us deeply miserable, but are restored to the favor of God, accepted in the Beloved, and have grace to overcome the world, the flesh, and the devil. The sanctifying Spirit to purge us from all filthiness is joined with this pardon, which delivers from the condemning guilt of sin. We are translated into the kingdom and family of Christ, as well as delivered from the kingdom of Satan and the power of darkness. In a word, the acceptance of our persons, the sanctification of our natures, the answer of our prayers, and a title to heaven and eternal life are connected with and consequent to the forgiveness of sin (Psalm 32:1–3; Zechariah 1:4; Isaiah 59:2–3; Psalm 103:2–3; Job 7:21).

This also has respect to all the comforts and afflictions of this present life. You ought to consider that, if sin is forgiven, all things shall work for good. "Take away all iniquity [said the church], and receive us graciously, or do us good" (Hosea 14:2). Every providence shall be sanctified if sin is forgiven. "For peace I had great bitterness," said Hezekiah, "but in love to my soul Thou hast delivered it from the pit of corruption; for Thou hast cast all my sins behind Thy back" (Isaiah 38:17). You have a like instance in Jeremiah 33:6–8. But if you had all the plenty, peace, health, riches, and grandeur of this world, yet the guilt of one sin on the conscience, under the apprehension of God's deserved wrath, will spoil the relish of all. Where sin is forgiven, other mercies will be sweet and the burden of affliction tolerable. But without this, and under the apprehensions of the contrary, every temporal calamity is double. For this is the wormwood and the gall in every bitter cup. We shall not, under the troubles and disappointments of this world, cry out that we are undone if we can think that God has forgiven us, any more than a man who has just received his prince's pardon (when he lays under a sentence of condemnation to death) can be thought, if he loses his glove or handkerchief on the way home, that he will wring his hands, weep, and take on for such a loss when he had so lately his life graciously given to him.

Besides, hereby a foundation is laid for a life of thankful love and obedience to God. Conscience being purged from dead works, we serve the living God without fear in hope of His acceptance, with the promise of His hearing our prayers, and that He will be well pleased with our services and overlook our infirmities. We may therefore well bear the trials of this life with patience and resignation; and in a dying hour shall be able to commend our souls with faith and hope into the hands of Christ, who will take care of us as His own when we leave the world, and at last publically acknowledge and absolve us in the great day. Oh, how many mercies accompany this mercy, that of the forgiveness of sin!

Fourth, this is mercy indeed to a returning sinner. It is peculiar mercy, as it is irrevocable. Where sin is forgiven and iniquity blotted out, it shall be remembered no more. You are freely justified from all things, and shall never come into condemnation. " 'My covenant of peace shall never be removed,' saith the Lord who hath mercy on thee' " (Isaiah 54:10). This is not only true of the first settlement of it, but is the priviledge of everyone who is under the bond and blessing of the New Covenant. "Though I visit his transgression with a rod, and his iniquity with stripes, nevertheless my lovingkindness will I not utterly take from him, nor suffer My faithfulness to fail. My covenant will I not break, nor alter the thing that is gone out of My lips" (Psalm 89:32–34). God may remember the sins of pardoned believers so as to afflict them in this world and exercise the discipline of His family. Their share in national sins may involve them in present sufferings with others. And for particular transgressions, God may testify His fatherly displeasure against good men by remarkable afflictions, but will not reverse their pardon so as to punish them eternally. Eli, David, Jonah, and others are examples. Your peace with heaven shall never be so broken; none of your afflictions will prove it. The reconciliation between God and sinners that is once accepted by a real, active, unfeigned, obedient faith is perpetual. It is promised that our iniquities shall be blotted out and remembered no more. God will cast them behind His back. He will cast them into the bottom of the sea and scatter them as a thick cloud (Isaiah 43:25; Psalm 51:9; Isaiah 38:17; Micah 7:19; Isaiah 44:22). And yet more expressly, to assure us that God will not enter into judgment with us for the sins He has once forgiven, we read in Jeremiah 50:20: "In that day shall the iniquity of Israel be sought for, and there shall be none; and the sins of Judah, and they shall not be found."

Where God bestows forgiveness, He communicates the spirit of grace for the mortification of sin. And though that work is not perfect, it shall be progressive; and the remainders of corruption in the soul will not prove that your sin is not forgiven. The flesh will war against the Spirit, and the Spirit will strive against the flesh; but you can't conclude that you are not forgiven from the opposition that sin makes against the grace of God in the soul. Would you judge yourselves? Consider what opposition you make against sin. Would you have relief? Apply to the open Fountain, to the blood and Spirit of Christ, for new strength from day to day to crucify the flesh, to continue the warfare and maintain the conflict. That sin yet remains in the soul is consistent with your reconciliation to God, and your sense of this with His acceptance of you. Yea, I am persuaded, there's never such a discovery of corruption as after forgiveness, when the grace of God has enlightened the soul. But which part do you side with? Do you condemn, bewail, oppose, resist, strive, watch, pray, fight, and endeavor the mortification of that corruption that yet remains after the hopes of pardon? You shall then, by the grace of Christ, hold on and be more than conquerors.

You should apply to Him and exalt His power, as able to destroy the works of the devil. He has promised, and undertaken it, that no iniquity shall be charged to your condemnation. No old stories shall be repeated, no latent displeasure harbored, and no former quarrel revived. If you return to God with all your heart, He will never upbraid you with your former sins, though men may. But if you can hope that God forgives you, you'll easily bear that, and little mind it. Can you doubt this fullness of pardon, when God has said that He will hide and blot out our sins so as, when sought for, they shall not be found, that He will put them as far from us as

the East is from the West, and that none of them shall
be mentioned again unto us (Psalm 103:10; Jeremiah
31:34).

Fifth, this pardoning mercy is mercy indeed to a returning sinner because all his unknown and forgotten
sins shall be pardoned as well as those he has particularly confessed, agravated, and repented of. As he who
breaks the law in one point is guilty of all, by the willful
contempt of divine authority, so he who is absolved in
one point is forgiven in all. It would otherwise be in
vain to be forgiven and absolved as to some sins that
might damn us, if there's any one left that would do it.
He who is under condemnation for one sin is liable to
eternal death, but divine forgiveness is entire and full.
There are sins of good men that arise from human
frailty, and not from any evil purpose of heart. Such are
as sins of ignorance, which, if we had known, we would
not have committed; or sins of sudden surprise, that we
did not observe, or fell into by the violent hurry of
temptation before we had time to think what we were
doing. Of such sins we shall often be guilty while we
are in the world, and we are bid to ask daily pardon for
them; and then they shall not break covenant between
God and us.

But there are many sins that we have forgotten for
which we were never humbled in particular. And yet, if
we truly repent of those we do know and call to mind,
our forgotten sins shall be forgiven. For God will
pardon us according to His own nature. He will forgive
us like a God, not according to our knowledge, but His
own. And as He is greater than our hearts, to know
much more against us than we can remember against
ourselves, so He is greater than our hearts, to forgive

even those faults which our hearts and consciences do not recollect. He knows the value of Christ's blood and merits to forgive all our sins. And, by unfeigned faith, we have an interest in the virtue of it. God has more thoughts of mercy in Him than we have had of rebellion against Him. Psalm 40:5: "Thy thoughts to usward [speaking of His thoughts of mercy] are more than can be numbered." They have been from everlasting, and reach to everlasting, whereas 'tis but as of yesterday that the oldest sinner began to rebel against God. There is no comparison.

And this leads to the last observation from those words: "He will abundantly pardon." God will not only show mercy to returning sinners so as to forgive them, but He will abundantly pardon. He will multiply forgivenesses.

The apostle speaks of the grace of our Lord Jesus Christ, that it was exceeding abundant towards him with the faith and love which are in Christ Jesus (1 Timothy 1:14). It is superlative, superabundant grace, not only sufficient for the pardon of his sins, but of multitudes more besides. In other places we read not only of the grace of God in forgiveness, but of His abounding grace, of the riches of His grace, yea, of the exceeding riches of His grace (Ephesians 1:6–7), and this is joined with tender mercies, with lovingkindness, and with multitudes of mercies.

Here I will show in what respects God will abundantly pardon returning sinners. We will then consider what reason we have to believe it and be firmly persuaded of it. We will then examine the abuse of this blessed doctrine, and then show in what respects God promises abundantly to pardon, or to multiply forgivenesses. And this I will show as to persons and as to things.

First, consider the extent of forgivenesses of sins with reference to time, place, and persons. Regarding time, from the first promise of the seed of the woman, made soon after the Fall, to the end of the world, this door of mercy is open for returning sinners. Regarding places, the gospel is appointed to be preached to every creature in every part of the world. Neither Jew nor Gentile, bond nor free, barbarian or Scythian, are excepted. The gospel of grace by Christ Jesus is everywhere the power of God to pardon, and it is salvation unto all who believe. Regarding persons, none shall perish for want of a sufficient price for their ransom, for want of a sufficient satisfaction to the justice of God. But wherever the everlasting gospel is preached, he who believes shall be saved. Whoever will may come and take of the waters of life freely. Whoever will accept the mercy of Christ, upon the holy terms of the gospel, shall receive remission of sins. John 3:16: "God so loved the [lost] world that whosoever believeth on Christ shall not perish, but have everlasting life." John 12:46–47: "I am come as a Light into the world, that whosoever believeth in Me should not abide in darkness. If any man hear My words and believe not, I judge him not; for I came not to judge the world, but to save the world." 1 John 2:2: "He is a propitiation for our sins, and not for ours only, but for the sins of the whole world."

And when we consider what sort of persons (even the chiefest and vilest of sinners) many of those have been who have been pardoned and received mercy, we must say that there is no respect of persons with God as to this matter. And there are great multitudes of these considered in themselves, for even of martyrs and confessors, who came out of great tribulation and had washed their robes, and made them white in the blood of the Lamb, there is a vast multitude, such as none could number, of all nations, kindreds, people, and tongues (Revelation 7:9, 14).

Second, He abundantly pardons, considering the sins forgiven. He is a God who pardons iniquity, transgression, and sins of all sorts. Let the kinds, numbers, repetitions, and aggravations be what they will. There is a multitude of tender mercies to forgive, and abundant virtue in the blood of Christ, to cleanse from all sin. If the multitude of transgressions could make a pile as high as from earth to heaven, God's pardoning mercy is above the heavens. His thoughts are above ours in this matter of forgiveness, as far as the heavens are above the earth. No sin but final impenitence, ungodliness, and unbelief are shut out from pardon; for the sin against the Holy Ghost is attended with that, and therefore is never to be forgiven.

As to sins after repentance and pardon, God has promised to multiply forgivenesses, to heal backslidings, and therefore He invites men to return, with a promise of pardon: "Return, ye backsliding children, and I will heal your backslidings." In some early days of the Christian Church, the Novatian doctrine spread that denies repentance and pardon to sins after baptism. Upon this account many good men delayed their baptism as long as they could so that they might not defile their garments after they were washed. It seemed to have risen from a misunderstanding of Hebrews 6:1. But any such doctrine as would discourage men's repentance, and returning to God after they have sinned, must be of very dangerous consequences to the souls of men.

I confess, it is a dismal symptom to fall often into willful sin; to repent and then sin again; to repent and sin in a circle. This argues an intention of sinning again rather than a design of leaving it. But for such as have returned to God and been forgiven, and yet by the power of temptation have afterwards fallen, there is great encouragement for their return, and grounds to hope for forgiveness. For "if any man sins, we have an Advocate with the Father, even Jesus Christ the Righteous," who was a propitiation for our sins. "If any man sins" is not meant to encourage to sin, but to prevent despair after the commission of it. And since we are to forgive one another, as God for Christ's sake has forgiven us, it would never have been made our duty to forgive our offending brother over and over, yea, unto seventy times seven, if there were no mercy with God for returning backsliders. You are allowed, and even commanded in such a case, to return to God and to sue for your pardon; and you ought to believe you shall find welcome, and that your backslidings shall be healed.

There is need of urging this, because sins after repentance, and after vows, resolutions, and sacraments, not only defile, but disturb the conscience; and you can't presently approach God with comfort. What then should you do? Give up all for lost? Run into excess of riot and say, "There is no hope; therefore let us walk after the imagination of our own hearts"? No, by no means. But by renewed acts of repentance towards God, and by faith in the blood of Jesus, return to God and seek forgiveness.

I grant that in such cases it is hard to do this with any encouragement and hope. Our hearts misgive us, and well they may. We shall have a thousand jealousies and fears, and it can't be otherwise. However, God's thoughts are not as ours. He will abundantly pardon returning sinners though you have abused His grace, though you have dishonoured His name, revolted after forgiveness, slighted the Redeemer Christ, grieved His Spirit, given advantage to the devil, and deserved to be cast out of His sight; though you have broken your solemn vows and broken your peace thereby—yet let such remember that God will show mercy to returning sinners, and He will abundantly pardon them. He will heal their backslidings, and make them loathe themselves and be confounded for all their abominations, even after He is pacified towards them (Ezekiel 16:63).

Note the kind language God used to Ephraim in Jeremiah 31:18, 20: "Surely I have heard Ephraim's bemoaning himself. He is My dear son; he is a pleasant child (or rather, is he not so?). Though I spake against him, I remember him still. My bowels are moved for him. I will surely have mercy on him." Read with thankfulness Micah 7:18–19: "Who is a God like unto Thee, that pardoneth iniquity, and passeth by the transgressions of His remnant, and retaineth not His anger forever, because He delighteth in mercy? He will turn again, and have compassion on us, and will subdue our iniquities and cast our sins into the depths of the sea."

How sweet is the repentance of such a returning backslider, that is kindly melted, humbled, and broken, and brought to the foot of God with hope of mercy through Christ? The contrition of such a soul is made up like that of Mary Magdalen, of tears and kisses, of sorrow and love, of humility and hope, of confusion and confidence, of shame and joy. And how will such a soul love much, to whom much is thus forgiven?

In short, God abundantly pardons, and multiplies pardons, as to the forgiveness of many sins, in that never any one sin was forgiven to any man to whom this was not made good. Numberless sins are forgiven wherever one is. They are more than the hairs of our head or the sands on the seashore. Well might the psalmist say, "Have mercy on me, O Lord, according to Thy lovingkindnesses, and according to the multitude of Thy tender mercies" (Psalm 51:1). "I will abundantly pardon," God says, and in another place, "I will cleanse them from all their iniquities, whereby they have sinned against Me, whereby they have trespassed against Me" (Jeremiah 33:8). Who can understand his errors before conversion and since, by omission and commission, in thought, in word, and in act? How long did God wait on some of us? What various methods did He use to bring us home? How graciously did He receive us at first, and, after many provocations, receive us again? Surely if we find mercy with God, any of us, He must abundantly pardon us and multiply forgivenesses.

And because 'tis not so easy a thing to believe this, I proceed to the second particular, to consider what reason we have to be persuaded of this.

Second, upon what grounds may we be firmly persuaded that God will thus multiply pardons? It is certain to a humbled, awakened, convinced, and penitent sinner; it must be glad tidings of great joy that his case will admit of hope, that he ought not to despair, that there is a possibility he may find mercy with God, if nothing more. But to have the riches of God's grace displayed, to have a free and general invitation made to all the hungry and thirsty, the weary and heavy-laden; to have a promise of mercy and of forgiveness, whatever your sins have been—what matter of rejoicing is this? This will answer a thousand objections, which otherwise you could not tell what to say to. This is proper to revive the most drooping spirits, to make them adore God and admire His glorious grace. This may cause them to think honorably of Him, to seek Him earnestly, and to thankfully accept His offered mercy, as poor, wretched, perishing, condemned, and undone creatures towards whom the God of all grace will magnify His rich and undeserved mercy. Therefore, be persuaded to believe it, considering such things as these:

First, there are large and express promises, and most astonishing instances, in the Holy Scriptures to encourage your faith. He who best understands His own kind thoughts to the children of men, to the chief of sinners, has assured you that He will not only have mercy, but will abundantly pardon; and that where sin has abounded, grace shall much more abound toward all who will accept mercy from Jesus Christ, so that God may not lose the glory of it. You think it very hard to be persuaded of this, but has not God told you that as far as the heavens are above the earth, so are His thoughts and ways above yours? Has He not told you that, though your sins be as crimson and scarlet, they shall be as snow and wool; and that to the Lord our God belong mercies and forgiveness, though we have rebelled against Him?

Have we not instances of the worst of men and women, who have been washed and justified through the blood and the Spirit of Christ, of sinks of sin who

have been made vessels of mercy? Are there not many
examples in the Old and New Testaments of Jews and
Gentiles? What folly, and what aggravated sin was David
guilty of after the knowledge of God? And what great
sins before conversion was the Apostle Paul charged
with? You have been sometimes told that 'tis an instance of God's wisdom and kindness to record the example of David's fall. Some, it may be, think it would be
better left out lest it should encourage sinners; but
doubtless many a man would have perished in despair,
and done away with himself, had it not been for the example of David's repentance, and God's forgiveness of
him, after such heinous transgressions.

Second, God has declared this to be His nature and
delight. He proclaims it as part of His name. Exodus
34:6–7 says that He is "the Lord God, gracious and merciful, slow to anger, and abundant in goodness and
truth, forgiving iniquity, transgression and sin." He is
pleased in the exercise of His mercy. He delights to be
gracious, and takes pleasure in them who hope in His
mercy. And therefore, what pleases Him, and what He
delights to do, He will do abundantly. There is an in-
exhaustible treasure of grace in God, exceeding riches
of grace, and unsearchable depths of mercy and grace.
"God, who is rich in mercy, for the great love wherewith
He loved us, even when we were dead in sins, hath
quickened us togther with Christ" (Ephesians 2:4–5).
All the saints are studious and thoughtful about the
glorious dimensions of God's grace, endeavoring to
comprehend the breadth, length, height, and depth of
this grace that passes knowledge (Ephesians 1:18–19).
The breadth of His love covers a multitude of sins and
pardons a multitude of sinners. The depth of it reaches

us in the depth of our sin and misery. The length of it is from everlasting to everlasting; the height of it raises us from a deserved hell to an infinitely glorious heaven. Love, grace, and mercy are His nature and delight. These above our thoughts and past our comprehension. We read that His judgments are unsearchable, and His ways past finding out; 'tis as true of His ways of mercy as of any others. By that name "judgments," His mercies are sometimes called. Psalm 36:6: "Thy judgments are a great deep." To show the meaning thereof, the psalmist breaks out: "O Lord, how excellent is Thy lovingkindness to the sons of men, that put their trust in Thee?" All the merits of Christ are called the mercies of God, and the sure mercies of David. God is said to be rich in mercy, and no other attribute of God is called His riches but His goodness, grace, and love.

Third, God uses a variety of arguments throughout Scripture to persuade us to believe this. He not only urges us from His own example, and obliges us to forgive our trespassing brother (if he repents) unto seventy times seven, but with the greatest kindness He bespeaks us to believe His compassion, to be persuaded of His tenderness and love. He employs a great deal of rhetoric to that purpose. "Why sayest thou, O Jacob, and speakest, O Israel, 'My way is hid from the Lord, and my judgment is passed over from my God?' Hast thou not known, hast thou not heard, that the everlasting God, the Lord, the Creator of the ends of the earth, fainteth not, neither is weary" (Isaiah 40:27–28)? He appeals to heaven and earth, to the dumb and insensible creatures, that His ways are equal, and that ours are unequal. He offers, He invites, He calls, expostulates, and complains of our backwardness to believe Him. He pleads and promises, and adds His oath to His Word: "As I live," says the Lord. In other words, "As I am a living God, I take no pleasure in the death of him who dies, but rather that he returns and lives than goes on and dies. Turn ye, turn ye, why will ye die, O house of Israel?" He is represented with sighs and groans, bewailing the obstinacy of sinners to their own destruction. "Oh, that they were wise, and would consider this! Oh, that there were such a heart in them! Oh, that they knew the things that belong to their peace before they are hidden from their eyes!" How kind and encouraging such passages are.

Fourth, this is one great end of God's patience and forbearance, and of His continuing the preaching of the Word and the ordinances of the gospel: that sinners might be led to repentance by the hopes of forgiveness. How many years has God waited on some of you? Should not the longsuffering of God, who has a tendency to salvation, encourage you to believe that there is mercy and forgiveness with Him? What quick dispatch has He made with others, while He has spared you? He has taken some in the act of their vile abominations; many in the very height of their wickedness, and has refused to give them further time and space to repent. He has called some to judgment in their youth, soon after they had broken the fetters of their education, cast off the God of their fathers, and begun to indulge themselves in youthful lusts. Many, you can be sure (not greater sinners than you) are gone to their place, while He yet waits to be gracious to you. He offers you pardon and life when He might have condemned you to remediless wrath, and put it to execution long ago. He continues to exercise great patience and power in forbearing with you.

Is it not with the kind design that it might lead you to repentance, that you might turn to Him, seek Him, and entreat His pity before it is too late? May you not infer this much from His longsuffering? Did He bear with you when your heart was as hard as a rock, and you would not hearken to any treaty of Peace? And will He not accept you now that your heart begins to be contrite and broken with a sense of sin and sorrow for it? Did He bear with you while sin was your delight, and will He not be gracious if you seek Him now that sin has become your burden? Does He continue to call you by His Word, and commission His ministers to tell you in His name that if you return He will abundantly pardon? Does He order them to beseech you for Christ's sake, and in His stead, that you would be reconciled to God? And can you suppose He is inexorable? If a king should send one of his attendants to a condemned prisoner, saying, "Go tell such a one, let him come to me for his pardon, and he shall have it; my son has interceeded for him, and made his peace, though he has forfeited his life and deserved to die, and I might put the sentence in execution tomorrow; yet let him come and confess his sin, and ask forgiveness, and I will pardon him. Yea, tell him that I desire, I entreat that he would come. I beg that he would have pity on himself and not refuse me. I earnestly pray and beseech him. I must take no denial; he must come." What kindness and condescension would this be! You know how to apply it. 'Tis as certain unto all of you, by the preaching of the gospel, as if you were spoken to by name.

But if you reject the kind offer of the grace of the gospel, and will not return from your evil ways, but go on and put it to the venture; (after such a merciful invitation, and that so often repeated), consider then what a hazard you run and, if you hold on, how dreadful your doom will be. All the ministers of Christ, instead of blessing you in the name of the Lord, must pronounce against you all the curses of the law, and all the additional curses denounced against the despisers of the gospel. They must say unto you, "Anathema, maranatha. Cursed in this world till the coming of Christ, and when He comes, accursed from His blessed presence into everlasting destruction." Yea, all the angels of God, all the churches of Christ, all the saints on earth and in heaven, will adore divine justice, and can have no compassion on you if you go on to despise the grace of God, and will not be drawn with the cords of His love.

Fifth, to persuade you that God will abundantly pardon, consider how valuable a price was paid for your redemption so that you might have forgiveness. When you think of the freeness of this mercy to you, think also that it cost the precious blood of Jesus to procure it. And, by the great propitiation for sin which He has made, God has glorified His holiness and justice, and may now glorify His mercy and grace in pardoning and saving sinners without lessening the honor of His authority and government, or impeaching any of His attributes and perfections. You may come and beg for mercy for the sake of Jesus Christ, saying, "Lord, save me for Thy mercy's sake. I am a vile sinner and a rebellious creature. I am not only an unprofitable servant, but a heinous criminal. I have nothing in myself but what is matter of shame and humiliation; nothing of any good but what Thou hast given me. There's nothing in any of my services but need the sprinkling of the

blood of Jesus to make them accepted. But there is redemption, even the forgiveness of sin through the
blood of Jesus. Lord, here is the blood shed for expia-
tion of my sins. Lord, here's the price paid for my reconciliation; here's a perfect righteousness to cover me;
here's a complete, atoning sacrifice. Christ's merit,
righteousness, intercession, and grace can save me.
Oh, let me be found in Him, accepted in Him! Did I
dishonor God formerly by my aggravated sins? Christ
my Redeemer has honored Him more by His death
than ever I dishonored Him by my wicked life."

Is it not a trouble to you to think with what affection
and delight you sinned, with what deliberation you
committed such and such sins? Oh, remember that
Christ delighted to do the mediatorial will of His
Father. He was straitened till He drank of the bitter
cup, and was baptized with His own blood. He knew be-
forehand all that He was to do and suffer for our redemption, and yet willingly undertook it. Did you sin
with much intenseness of spirit, so that your heart was
in it? Have your crimes been (many of them) mental,
spiritual, inward sins (like those of the devil, which are
worse than sensual, carnal ones)? Remember, Christ's
sufferings lay much in His soul also. His spirit, His soul
was heavy unto death.

And whatever unworthiness you may apprehend of
the mercy offered to you, remember that it is free
mercy. You are called and invited to receive it without
money and without price. If you are weary and heavy-
laden, and sensible of your unworthiness; if you see
your need of His help, are desirous of it, and willing to
yield yourselves to His conduct, to be saved in a way of
free grace, so as to give Him the entire glory of your

salvation, you ought to believe that God will show you mercy, and will abundantly pardon you. He has glorified His mercy in the purchase of forgiveness by Christ, in the publication of it in the gospel, and in the application of it to particular sinners upon faith and repentance, or repentance and faith. I will not worry about which I put first, since they are inseperable, and are never parted. Both are absolutely needful: repentance towards God, and faith in our Lord Jesus Christ, so that at once we may give God the honor of His authority and violated law by our repentance, and of His rich grace in the gospel by our faith in Christ. And can anything be more free to us than to be forgiven, in this method and on these terms, to have all our transgressions blotted out for His name's sake, and to be washed and cleansed in the fountain of Christ's blood, when we have nothing but our own miserable and wretched case to move His pity? He justifies us freely by His grace, and found a way to do it with honor to His own name.

What a strange passage is that in Isaiah 43:22–24: "Thou hast not called upon Me, O Jacob, but hast been weary of Me, O Israel. Thou hast not brought Me the small cattle of thy burnt offerings, neither hast thou honored Me with thy sacrifice; thou hast brought Me no sweet cane with money, neither hast thou filled Me with the fat of thy sacrifices, but thou hast made Me to serve with thy sins. Thou hast wearied Me with thine iniquities."

What might now be expected but that God should say, "Therefore I will not hear you when you call. I'll make you a sacrifice to My wrath. I'll punish you according to what you deserve." But it is quite otherwise, for it follows in verse 25: "I, even I, am He that blotteth out thy transgressions for My own sake, and will not remember thy sins." When the God whom we had offended by sin has become a God of forgiveness in such a way and method of rich and glorious grace, we need not doubt that His heart is in it, and therefore that He will abundantly pardon. He might have exacted the punishment of sin when He gave His only begotten Son to be a propitiation for our sin, and accepted His suffering instead of ours. Nothing could move Him to this but His own grace and love. And therefore we ought to believe that He is ready to receive returning sinners unto mercy for Christ's sake.

Sixth, consequent to this, consider that by believing that God will abundantly pardon returning sinners we give honor and glory to God. He is pleased and honored by our giving credit to His Word, and by hoping in His mercy, whereas, if we distrust His promises and declarations of grace, we not only disobey His order, but refuse that which He delights in, and whereby He is glorified. By not believing His promises of pardon, we do what we can to frustrate the command of faith in Jesus Christ, and the promise of salvation by Him, yea, to disappoint the great design of Christ's coming into the world, which was to save sinners. We undervalue the rich provision He has made for our encouragement; we gratify the devil in keeping away from the only remedy which Christ has procured. In effect, we make God a liar by disbelieving the record He has given of His Son, not setting to it our seal that God is true (1 John 5:10; John 3:33). If we honor and please God by our faith and hope more than by anything else, we do as much dishonor and displease Him by our unbelieving despondency and despair. Yea, all the sins of your past life, that make you afraid that God will never forgive you, are not clothed with higher aggravations of guilt than your doubting the pardon of them if you unfeignedly return to God and believe in Christ.

Last, you ought to believe it for the reason added in verse 7, because God's thoughts are not as ours, but are as far as the heavens are above the earth. We can't think so kindly of any who have injured us as God thinks of us who have offended Him; nor can we think to what degree God is able to forgive our greatest provocations, and show mercy to the vilest sinners who will return. We are prone to revenge, and are not easily reconciled; we are apt to return evil for evil; we are not easily brought to forgiveness. But "My thoughts are not as yours," said God. "You do not know how far My mercy can reach. I am God, and not man. The distance between God and man, between the creature and Creator, is infinitely more than between heaven and earth. So what if you can't imagine that ever I should have such thoughts of mercy for poor sinners. Do you consider how high the heavens are above the earth? So are My thoughts and ways higher than yours. They are like Myself: infinite."

How many, by their own experience of God's kind and gracious dealing with them, with holy wonder and thankfulness, have acknowledged and attested the truth of this?

> Many a time have I called myself a prodigal, a companion of swine, a miserable, hard-hearted sinner, unworthy to be called His son, when He has called me "child," and chided me for questioning His love. He has readily forgiven the sins which I

thought would have made my soul the fuel of hell. He has entertained me with joy, with music and a feast, when I better deserved to have been among the dogs outside His doors. He has embraced me in His sustaining, consolatory arms when He might have spurned my guilty soul to hell, and said, "Depart from Me, thou worker of iniquity. I know thee not." Oh, little did I think that He could ever have forgotten the vanity and villany of my youth, yea, so easily have forgotten my most aggravated sins. When I had sinned against light, when I had resisted conscience, when I had frequently and willfully injured love, I thought He would never have forgotten it; but the greatness of His love and mercy, and the blood and intercession of His Son has cancelled all. Oh, how many mercies have I tasted since I thought I had sinned away all mercies! How patiently He has borne with me since I thought He would never have put up with more? Though I injure and dishonor Him by loving Him no more, though I often forget Him, and have been out of the Way when He has come or called me; though I have disobediently turned away my ears, unkindly refused the entertainments of His love, and unfaithfully played with those whose company He forbade me—yet He has not divorced me or turned me out of doors.

Oh, wonderful, that heaven will be familiar with earth, and God with Man! The Highest with a worm, and the Most Holy with an unconstant sinner! Man refuses me when God will entertain me: Those whom I never wronged reject me with reproach, and God, whom I have unspeakably injured, invites me, entreats me, and condescends to me, as if He were beholden to me to be saved. Men of whom I have deserved well abhor me, and God, from whom I have deserved hell accepts me. I upbraid myself with my sins, but He does not upbraid

me with them. I condemn myself for them, but He
does not condemn me. I have peace with Him before I can have peace with my conscience. [Taken
from *The Divine Life*, Part 3: "Of Conversing With
God in Solitude," p. 873, found in volume 3 of *The
Practical Works of Richard Baxter.*]

OBJECTION. "But after all these endearing expressions of the grace of God," some may say, "We can't tell
how to believe. 'Tis hard to be fully persuaded of this."

ANSWER. Consider therefore the verses following
our text, where this objection is obviated. You say that
you can't have your hearts duly affected with these declarations of God's grace, that you can't be brought to
accept this mercy, to close with this offer, or to be encouraged by such a promise and trust in it. Therefore
verses 10–11 are added, as being directly suitable to
such a case: "As the rain cometh down, and the snow
from heaven, and returneth not thither, but watereth
the earth, and maketh it bring forth and bud, that it
may give seed to the sower and bread to the eater, so
shall My Word be that goeth forth out of My mouth; it
shall not return unto Me void, but it shall accomplish
that which I please; it shall prosper in the thing
whereto I sent it." That is, "As the heavens do not give
light, heat, or snow in vain, but cause a promising
spring and a fruitful harvest, so," says God, "My
thoughts of grace, manifested by My declarations of
mercy and promises of forgiveness, shall have efficacy
and influence to make you believe, to enable you to
hope and trust in my mercy, and so to be quiet and satisfied that your great and heinous sins shall be forgiven. The very publication of this grace shall be attended with a power to bring souls to believe it. I know

My thoughts toward you are thoughts of peace, and not of evil; to give you a gracious end, and raise your expectations of it, and they shall accordingly be fulfilled. The declarations of this mercy shall be credited. My word of grace shall not be in vain; it shall take hold of dejected, despairing souls and raise them to faith and hope."

It is with this encouragement that we publish the glad tidings of salvation, and invite sinners to return to God by Jesus Christ, with an assurance of finding mercy. I say, 'tis with this encouragement that we beseech them to be reconciled to God, and assure them that He is ready to forgive. 'Tis in hope that, by the Spirit accompanying the declaration of the Word concerning this forgiveness with God, many souls might be attracted and won, persuaded and overcome, and so prevailed with to return to God and believe the glorious riches, freeness, and abundance of His mercy. God grant that we may find, more and more, such fruits of preaching the gospel. On the other hand, I beseech you to take heed how you turn your backs on this mercy of God, and the offer of it. Beware how you shut your ears against His gracious invitation, when He thus proclaims and publishes His readiness to forgive. Take heed how you go on in sin after God freely offers you the forgiveness of all your sins if you will return. With the greatest seriousness I must tell you that one such sermon of God's forgiving grace and mercy rejected, slighted, or misimproved may be of more dreadful consequence to the souls of those who hear it and make light of it than I am able to express.

Application

USE 1. Let this mercy, love, and grace overcome your hearts. Consider it again and again. Apply it seriously to yourselves. Is the Lord this gracious to me after so long a rejection of Him? Will He yet receive me after so many refusals? Does He invite and call me again after so much contempt of His mercy and grace? Will He yet show mercy to me? What strange, astonishing grace, what endearing kindness is this? What manner of love is this? How true is it that God's thoughts and ways are not as ours that God should speak such language to me as this. "Though for lying vanities you have forsaken your own mercies, yet return to Me. Though you have played the harlot with many lovers, yet return. Though you have turned a deaf ear to many reproofs, yet your case is not desperate. I offer My Son, and life by Him ("He that hath the Son hath life"), and you would not: This offer was repeated sabbath after sabbath for many years, yet you would not hear it; you would not stoop to the terms; yet return unto Me. I will pity and pardon you abundantly. Long since I might have sworn in My wrath that you shall never enter into My rest. I might have said, 'Let them alone, to be undone by their own obstinate, foolish choices.' I might have resolved that never such an offer would be made to you again. Never any sermon about it shall do you good again, but I am God, and not man. My thoughts and ways are not as yours. I invite you again. I beseech you to turn and live; do not go on and die."

God speaks this language to every one of you, the worst of you, who hear me this day. Let none therefore think or say that it is too late for him or her, that there's now no more mercy for them. For Christ yet stands at the door and knocks; though you have refused formerly, and shut the door formerly, yet now, if you will open the door, He will come in and sup with you, and you with Him (Revelation 3:20). Nay, though He has not taken possession of your heart, He knocks at your door by His Spirit and is ready to enter. Though you refuse Him, He does not abandon you. Though His kindness and love have been slighted, yet His mercy is still offered and His patience is prolonged. And will you resolve to go on thus? Will you not return? Are you content to perish rather than come to Christ for life, rather than give Him the glory of your salvation? Will you rather die in your sins than be beholden to Him for your forgiveness, rather than apply to God for it when He has provided an all-sufficient Savior, and offered you that salvation freely which cost Him so dear to purchase? After this, for a poor, proud sinner to turn his back upon this grace of God, to scorn this Savior and disdain to be saved by Him, saying in effect, "I will have none of your Christ, none of His grace, none of His mercy. I would rather enjoy my lusts, continue in my sin, and put it to the venture," how provoking is such guilt? And how righteous will be the condemnation of such obstinate sinners?

USE 2. Apply yourself therefore to God in Christ by earnest prayer. He has the words of eternal life. He is a Prince and a Savior, to give repentance as well as pardon. The spirit of faith is the Spirit of Jesus Christ. He can open your blind eyes and soften your hard heart. He who commanded the cripple to take up his bed and walk, at the same time gave him power to obey. There is a divine Spirit and power, even the Spirit of life and power in Christ Jesus, that accompanies the preaching of the gospel. This may be hoped for, and this ought to be valued, desired, and begged for. You ought never to despair of God's grace to enable you to believe when it continues to be your duty to believe on Christ; and it cannot but continue to be so unless the gospel is repealed. Therefore, beg with all your hearts that you may be enabled to look to Him and be saved; to come to Him and find rest for your souls; to believe on Him and receive remission of sins. For by beholding the glory of God in the face of Christ, you may be changed into the same image, from glory to glory.

Beg for an understanding to know Him who is true, and with all your hearts to believe on Him so that you may assent to His Word, consent to His covenant, resign yourselves to His will, and trust in His promise, depending on His readiness, willingness, power, and faithfulness to save you. Say, "Lord, draw me, and I will run after Thee. Lord, Thou art willing to receive sinners; make me willing to receive Thee. Lord, Thou hast received gifts for men, even for the rebellious; Oh, communicate those gifts of grace to me! I see my need of Christ, and what reason I have to come to Him. Oh, lead me to Him, and work in me to will and to do of Thine own good pleasure!"

USE 3. If you begin to find the Spirit of Christ breathing on your souls, that have been yet unpersuaded; if you have any motions of the good Spirit of God by the preaching the Word, or by any other means, take heed that you thankfully cherish and entertain them. When you find your souls beginning to turn towards Christ, if you find any beams of heavenly light breaking in upon you, any inclinations started of applying to Him, be sure to obey the voice of His Spirit. Open every door of your souls to receive His light. When He works any conviction of sin, any sense of your need of a Savior, any desires after Him, or purposes of heart to leave your sins, and give yourselves up to God, to be saved by Christ according to the gospel—for your soul's sake, encourage such thoughts and cherish such suggestions. Beware how you turn them off, but presently and thankfully say, "Lord, I yield. I am over-come. I have long enough, and too long refused Thy grace, disobeyed Thy will, and resisted Thy Spirit. Thou hast often knocked, and I would not open. Oh, now enter, Thou Blessed of the Lord, and take possession of my soul! Let Christ dwell in my heart by faith, and let His Spirit form a temple there, and reside there as in His own dwelling forever. Lord, art Thou yet willing, after all my provocations, to show mercy, and abundantly to pardon? Art Thou yet willing to be my God and my Savior? Blessed be God, I am now willing to be Thy ser-vant. Thy powerful grace has made me willing. Thy Spirit opened my eyes to see myself undone, to see that Christ is able and willing to save me. I am now ready to receive Him, willing to embrace Him as Christ Jesus my Lord. I come to Thee, O God, as to the Fountain of Life, to be quickened and cleansed, to be washed, justified, sanctified, and saved from sin and hell by the blood and Spirit of Jesus, through the free mercy and grace of God."

To conclude, if after all there are any such here as are not or will not be persuaded to forsake their evil ways and turn to God in Christ, let them consider that the longer they continue in their obstinacy and unbe-lief under the preaching of the glorious grace and mercy of God to sinners, so much the more danger they are in of being lost forever, for their minds must be more blinded by sinning against the light. Their hearts are more hardened by misimproving that which should have softened them. The power of conscience is weakened after so many strugglings and combats that they must have had with their own consciences, after so many contests between corruption and conviction, between truth in the mind and corrupt inclinations in the heart, especially if they have formerly been awakened, and there have been some fears and hopes, with good desires and other affections formerly stirred. If by the common operations of the Holy Spirit they have had some serious concern about their salvation, and all this is worn off and gone, the case of such is very bad, and their recovery the less hopeful, because their repentance is the more unlikely. And if they persist, their doom will be intolerable. But it is to prevent this that, to those who may be in such a dangerous case, I thus speak. And therefore I most earnestly invite, beseech, and entreat them, however wicked and unrighteous they have been, not to make light of this further offer of the grace of the gospel. I desire that by no means they would despair of finding mercy with God, even now, if they will return to Him with all their hearts, whatever their past sins have been. If now they will return, God will abundantly pardon, for His thoughts are not as ours.

3

The Application of the Doctrine

"Let the wicked forsake his way, and the unrighteous man his thoughts, and let him return unto the Lord, and He will have mercy upon him; and to our God, for He will abundantly pardon." Isaiah 55:7

In the two previous chapters I have considered this double precept, or injunction of duty, which concerns sinners of all sorts; under the two names of "wicked" and "unrighteous," that they must forsake their evil ways and thoughts and return to the Lord, which are the two parts of unfeigned repentance. I have also considered the encouraging promise that thereupon God will have mercy and will abundantly pardon.

There remains something of the application of the second general point, that if the wicked forsake their evil ways and thoughts, and return to God, He will not only forgive, but He will abundantly pardon.

USE 1. Be thankful to heaven for the good news that God will thus mercifully treat returning sinners. He might have insisted on the terms of the violated first covenant to the ruin of all mankind. He might have left us, as He did the fallen angels, without the proposal, promise, or offer of a Redeemer. But "God so loved the world that He gave His only begotten Son, that whosoever believeth on Him should not perish, but have everlasting life."

When we think of the case of the fallen angels, who are reserved in chains of darkness to the judgment of the Great Day, and compare it with our own, who have a proclamation of mercy and grace by the gospel, we have reason to adore the distinguishing goodness of God to us. If a few poor, inconsiderable people in a kingdom, of the meanest sort, should be found guilty of treason against a prince; when there are multitudes of the nobility and gentry who have likewise rebelled against Him; and a pardon should be offered to those of the poorer, meaner sort, while the nobles and great men are all executed, and not a man of them received to mercy, would not this be astonishing goodness to the others? Especially if those great men, the principal subjects of the kingdom, were condemned for one offense for one act of treason, and the others forgiven many transgressions, and received to favor and honor after many years of rebellion. You easily know how to apply it.

How thankful ought we to be that we are not left in the remediless condition of devils, that there is a sacrifice offered for sin, a full atonement made, a sufficient price paid, a fountain opened, a new and living way for God to be glorified in the forgiveness and salvation of returning sinners who believe on His Son. It is a matter of continual admiration and thankful praise that we have forgiveness this way. Can we have a fuller evidence of the evil and malignity of sin, or of God's displeasure against it (and, consequently, of the worth and value of a pardon) than by the sufferings, blood, and sacrifice of Christ? And what stronger proof, or clearer evidence of God's readiness to forgive sin, than giving His Son to die for our sins, to cleanse us from all sin, even the most heinous, grievous offenses, because His mercy through the Mediator is greater than the sins of the whole world.

Let us with hearty thankfulness adore Him for this glorious mystery of His love and grace. And, that we may be thankful indeed, let us apply it to ourselves in particular. Let us think of our own miserable case under the guilt of sin and the curse of God. Let us think of the many thousands of talents we owe, without being able to pay one farthing, of the innumerable crimes we are guilty of, and that the wages of every one of them is death, that all the creatures in heaven and earth could not procure the forgiveness of one sinful thought. If you think you have, or ever had, any serious sense of the evil of sin, and your lost, undone condition as sinners, how thankfully would you receive these glad tidings of mercy by Jesus Christ? But if you have gone further, and have actually received the atonement; if you are brought under the bond of the covenant; if you are united to Christ by faith, and so interested in the sure mercies of David, and by forgiveness delivered from condemnation—what special thankfulness is due from such, when there are comparatively so few to whom the gospel is preached, but do receive this grace of God in vain? "Lord, who and what am I, that I should have good hope through grace of the forgiveness of my sins, that have been more aggravated than the sins of others; when others, not greater sinners (it may be, not so bad) shall perish forever, and never be forgiven; when it may be that some of my companions, and accomplices in sin, are cut off by death, without repentance and pardon! Were not others called and invited as well as I? But He has opened my ears and heart to receive Him; and so has pardoned me, while others are condemned. Oh, admirable and astonishing grace!"

USE 2. Take heed of abusing this declaration of grace to the worst of sinners.

1. Shall we sin because God is ready to forgive sin, so that His grace may abound? God forbid (Romans 6:1). Far be it from us; let it be an abhorred thought. It is needful to mention this because, in many instances, the most pure and holy doctrine may be perverted to patronize sin. We read that the continuance of the course of nature was made a ground of trust by the psalmist, as an adorable evidence and instance of His faithfulness and truth. Psalm 119:89: "Thy Word is settled in the heavens, and Thy faithfulness to all generations." And yet some atheistically abused it, 2 Peter 3:4, saying, "All things continue as they were. Where is the promise of His coming?" The apostle says, "The time is short, and the fashion of the world passes away." Therefore, let them who have such and such relations, possessions, and employments in the world, "carry it as if they had none. While others abuse this and say, "The time is short; let us eat and drink, for tomorrow we may die." So here, God is ready to show mercy to returning sinners. Therefore, "Let the wicked forsake his way. . . ."

Others turn this grace of God into wantonness, and will venture more boldly upon sin because God is ready to forgive. The Apostle John said, "These things I write unto you that ye sin not. But if any man sin, we have an Advocate with the Father, Jesus Christ the Righteous." There's a vast difference between the remission of sins past and an allowance of sin for the future. We may take comfort in the abounding grace of God, and His readiness to forgive—though we must dread the thought of

venturing on sin that His grace may abound in the forgiveness of it. This is contrary to all gratitude and in-
genuity, and to the true nature of faith and repentance.
And there can hardly be a more dangerous symptom of
damnable ungodliness than for any to presume to sin
upon the consideration that they hope they shall be
forgiven. The Apostle Jude (verse 4) speaks of some
"who turn the grace of God into wantonness, denying
the only Lord God, and our Lord Jesus Christ." He says
that these were ordained of old to condemnation: "For
the grace of God that brings salvation ought to teach us
to deny ungodliness and worldly lusts."

Sinning against God because He will abundantly
pardon is in some respects more aggravated than the
sin of devils, who will curse God and fly in His face, because there's no hope of pardon. But God offers pardon
to you, and declares that He is ready to forgive. And will
you dare to sin the more? If ever you are awakened to a
sense of sin, this of all others will be most likely to sink
you into despair, that you ventured to sin in hopes of
pardon. For what can relieve a convinced, awakened
soul but the free grace of God in the forgiveness of sin?
Whereas such a one may say, "Lord, this very mercy I
have abused: I have sinned the more because of this
grace." And if we should mention to such a one the instances of Manasseh, Paul, and others, who after great
sins were pardoned, he will be ready to reply that they
never sinned in hope of forgiveness, or turned the
grace of God into wantonness, as I have done.

There's forgiveness with God that He may be feared,
served, loved, and obeyed. But will any say, "There's forgiveness with God that He may be slighted and neglected, rebelled against, and disobeyed?" His abused

goodness will turn to more intolerable wrath against all such as presume on His mercy, apprehending that they shall find an easy pardon though they continue in their sins. It is to sin against the very nature and end of God's grace, to cut off their own plea for it, and the general ground of their hope in it. It is without a promise, and against a threatening, for any to expect forgiveness if they willfully continue in sin. It is to pervert the whole gospel to imagine that God will justify the ungodly while they remain in their unbelief and ungodliness. Is not unbelief a part of ungodliness, as being contrary to the most express command of God to believe on His Son? If ever God shows mercy unto any, and abundantly pardons them, He always gives them repentance unto life, and faith unfeigned.

And let such remember that, as God promises mercy and forgiveness to returning sinners, and that His thoughts are as far above ours as heaven is above the earth in this matter, so His thoughts of anger, wrath and fury against obstinate, willful, presumptuous, impenitent sinners are also above our thoughts, as far as the heavens are above the earth. He will tear in pieces, and none shall deliver. He who made them will show them no mercy; and who knows the power of His anger? He will laugh at their calamity, and mock when their fear comes. He will wound the head of His enemies, and the hairy scalp of such a one who goes on still in his trespasses (Proverbs 1:26; Psalm 68:21).

2. Take heed of abusing this doctrine of God's grace by admitting slight thoughts of sin, so as to encourage you to delay seeking after forgiveness, or to seek and expect it in any other way but through faith in Jesus Christ.

As to the matter of delay, the uncertainty of life, and the uncertainty of God's giving grace hereafter to those who refuse it now is sufficient to be said here, if duly considered. That which I now aim at is to discourage any hopes of obtaining forgiveness with God but through the blood, sacrifice, and righteousness of Christ: There is no other Savior, no other Mediator between God and man. If ever you are reconciled to God and find mercy with Him, it must be through Jesus Christ. The way and method is fixed and published, and declared to be unalterable. There is no other name under heaven but His by which any man can be saved. If God is gracious to any, and delivers them from going down to the pit, it is because He has found a ransom (Job 33:24).

The absolute mercy of God is not to be rested in, for He has told us in what way and method He will dispense His mercy, and how we shall partake of it. We must honor the Son as we honor the Father; receive Him as Christ Jesus the Lord, the only Mediator between God and man; and if we do not believe that Jesus is He, we must die in our sins. It is not enough to cease to do evil, and make restitution where you have injured and wronged any (which yet is a necessary fruit of repentance); it is not a little outward reformation, or the performance of some duties of religious worship that before were neglected that will be sufficient, if you overlook Jesus Christ, and lay the stress of your hope for acceptance with God on anything else.

If you should fast, pray, weep, mourn, wear sackcloth, give all you have to the poor, and continue in a life of austerity and mortification for many years, this will not avail, if you think to pacify God herewith, and substitute this for the blood and righteousness of Christ in order to obtain forgiveness. You will but provoke God, dishonor the Redeemer, and deceive your own souls. We are naturally prone to fix on some other foundation and are inclined to establish a righteousness of our own instead of Christ Jesus and His righteousness. But we can never be secure from the charge of the condemning law, and the challenge of divine justice, but by being united to Christ, interested in Him, found in Him, and accepted with God on His account.

USE 3. Let me beseech you to pity those sinners who have not returned to God and are not interested in His pardoning mercy; pity such as, desiring and endeavoring to return, yet apprehend and fear that they shall never be pardoned.

As for those who are yet under the guilt of sin, and have not returned to God, nor are interested in His pardoning mercy, consider their miserable case and pity them. And here are reasons for this pity:

First, if they are not partakers of this abundant pardon, there's no one sin that they were ever guilty of that is forgiven. Without repentance (which includes forsaking our evil ways, and returning to God), there's no forgiveness of any sin. Though temporal judgments have sometimes been diverted upon external humiliation, no one sin is blotted out but through the blood of Christ, who is exalted to be a Prince and Savior, to give repentance as well as remission of sins—and these are never to be parted. Therefore, if any of you have lived twenty, thirty, or forty years in the world, or longer, whenever God comes to enter into judgment with you, all the sins of your past life, with all their several aggravations, will be found in the indictment, and charged against you. You are under the guilt of them all as much as if they were committed yesterday. As God's pardoning mercy reaches to all the unknown and forgotten sins of true penitents, as well as those which they actually remember and repent of, so where He does not forgive all, He forgives none. And if the guilt of one sin is enough to sink you into hell, what is it to have ten thousand to answer for? If you can't stand in the judgment when accused but for one sinful thought or word, what will become of you when you have all the numberless transgressions of your past life to answer for?

Second, consider that, till sin is forgiven, the guilt of every unpardoned sinner increases every day. The longer he lives, he is still heaping up wrath against the day of wrath. Upon every failure of our duty to God or man, there's a debt of punishment resulting from it; and every new sin is a figure added to the old score. The longer therefore anyone lives in an unpardoned state, the more guilt he contracts, and the more crimes he has to answer for.

Third, consider that, upon this account, till we are interested in the pardoning mercy of God, we are under the curse and condemnation of the law. Whatever advantages a man may enjoy above others, whatever gifts, reputation, prosperity, he's still under a divine curse. He's condemned already, and if he dies in this condition he must perish forever. And how soon may death put a period to all your hopes of forgiveness? In the meantime, you are under a divine curse that reaches to all you have and all you enjoy, in health and sickness, prosperity and adversity, wherever you go and whatever you do. You please God in nothing, but abuse His mercy and are liable every moment to His wrath; and if you die, that stroke of death which separates your soul from your body will separate you from God and heaven forever.

This curse of God will be found to be intolerable as well as unavoidable. When God deals with sinners as a God of vengeance, they shall not be so weak as to be annihilated by His wrath, or so strong as to resist or avoid His righteous vengeance. It is everlasting wrath likewise: without being now reconciled to God, and interested in His pardoning mercy by Jesus Christ, the wrath of God abides on you, and will forever abide.

Fourth, let me add one more consideration to raise your pity to unpardoned sinners, and that is their present deplorable case by the accusations of their own conscience. For sooner or later a guilty conscience will speak, especially to those who live under the preaching of the gospel. Sinners in Zion shall be afraid; fearfulness shall surprise the hypocrite. They may try various methods to stop the mouth of conscience by the noise and clatter and hurry of worldly business; they may think to forget their misery and patch up a kind of peace for a little while; but this is a false peace that, if not speedily broken, will end in everlasting anguish. And if it is (as a thousand to one but it will be), what trembling, horror, and despair must be expected? How low will such sink when they awake out of their security? How will they roar and cry out under the terrors of the Lord? How bitterly will they complain of the burden of sin as a mountain on their backs, of the wounds of sin as so many poisoned arrows in their hearts? How will their joints tremble, their lips quiver, and their hearts ache when they shall see their sins set in order before them, and can't hope for pardon? But whether they feel their misery or not, their case is dismal, for they merely dance about the bottomless pit, and the next hour may tumble in. Conscience may awake sooner than you believe, and ere long it will. Conscience, I say, which is an accuser, none can silence; it is a judge that none can bribe. And if they will but give themselves time and leisure to think; a gloomy darkness, like the shadow of death, must now overspread their souls. They have no relief but by endeavoring not to think of their danger. Are not such to be pitied? Oh, do what you can to awaken and save them!

There's another sort who need your compassion: they who desire and endeavor to return to God, and seek after Christ, but apprehend there is no forgiveness for them. Though God will abundantly pardon others, they reckon they shall never gain an interest in His pardoning mercy. They hear of God's multiplying forgivenesses to others, but dare not think that they shall have a share in it. They read of a Savior, but believe they shall never be saved by Him; they hardly dare look into the Bible lest they read their own condemnation. All the terrible things in the Scriptures against impenitent unbelievers, against apostates and obstinate sinners, they do not apply to themselves. They dare not look into the grave, nor think of dying, because of what follows in the final judgment of Christ and the everlasting destruction of sinners. If they had any former peace, they reckon it was all deceit, mistake, and presumption. For after all their profession, hearing, reading, and praying, they tell you that they shall perish and be condemned as hypocrites, and there's no mercy for them.

Oh, with what bowels of pity and compassion should we consider the case of such, and treat them with the spirit of meekness and gentleness! "Christ is the Savior of sinners, but He is not mine," they say, "for I heard His gospel grace declared, but did not accept it. I outstood my day of grace, and the things of my peace are hidden from my eyes. He called me, but I would not come; and 'tis now too late. Oh, 'tis now too late! He knocked and I would not open, and now the door is shut against me. I am given up to a hard heart."

The very thought of heaven and the happiness of the saints only terrifies them because they think they have lost it and shall never come there, as well as the thoughts of hell, which they reckon to be their deserved portion, and that ere long it will be so. That word "everlasting," as in everlasting destruction, cuts them to the heart. And well it may, if they believe it belongs to them, and that they shall fall under the condemning sentence of the Judge to pass into everlasting fire. In several such cases, the Devil strikes in and aggravates their distress. He insults over them. "What do you now think of sin? Where's the pleasure and advantage of it now? To what purpose has been all your praying, hearing, attending on ordinances, and coming to the Lord's Table? You are fit indeed to come to the Lord's Table. You have come unworthily; you have sealed your damnation by it; you have eaten and drank judgment to yourselves by it again and again."

Such is their darkness and perplexity that they do not know what to answer, but conclude that they are lost and the gospel is hidden from them; that Christ is not their Friend, and will not be their Savior. Some of them will tell you that they are as sure of it, as if they were in hell already. 'Tis as true, they say, as if they had heard His condemning sentence. He has shut up His compassion and His tender mercy forever from them. Nothing remains but a fearful looking for wrath, judgment, tribulation, and anguish. And all their present darkness is but the forerunner of eternal darkness. What they feel now is nothing to what they fear. And if they are in such agonies now, what will it be to lie in the flames of hell? Wretched, miserable creatures! They do not know how to live, and they dare not die, lest death should open the door to eternal damnation. And these fears are heightened when ever they meet with those Christians who have any hopes of heaven. Do not such as these deserve our compassion? (And there are many such in this city.) Though natural melancholy and bodily indisposition give some occasion, at least to heighten such terrors and distress in several, yet the sense of past guilt and the temptations of Satan must not be overlooked.

What I have to say on the third general point of God's thoughts not being as ours will be suitable to their case. But before I proceed to that, let me mention something to help us try and examine ourselves whether we are interested in this forgiveness or not?

Would you know whether your sins are forgiven, whether you have an interest in this promise of multiplied pardon? Consider in the general, and examine your repentance towards God, and faith in our Lord Jesus Christ (Acts 2:21). See the sermons on the forgiveness of sin by the Reverend Dr. William Bates, where the whole doctrine of pardon is more accurately laid down [contained in volume 2 of *The Works of William Bates,* published by Sprinkle Publications]. The essential acts of repentance are godly sorrow for all our known sins; and a sincere purpose of heart to turn from all sin to God, with answerable endeavors of universal holiness. The three acts of saving faith in Christ are (1) an assent of the mind to Scripture revelation concerning Christ; (2) the consent of the soul, embracing and receiving Him upon His own terms; and (3) a reliance and trust on Him for pardon of sin and eternal life.

More particularly, consider your repentance and inquire how you stand affected to sin? Have you been under any deep conviction of the evil of sin so as to cause not only some sorrow, but hatred and detestation of it? Have you seen yourselves lost and undone by reason of guilt, so as absolutely to need pardoning mercy? Is the heart of stone taken away and a heart of flesh given? What humiliation for sin, and self-abasement in the apprehension of your vileness, have you ever had? Have you been disquieted and burdened under the sense of sin so as to condemn yourselves, and see that you are lost without the free mercy of God in Christ, owning the righteousness of God, if He should cast you off, and yet looking up to God through Jesus Christ with hope? 'Tis true, there is a great difference in the expressions of sorrow and humiliation for sin, which some make beyond others, but all are made to see the evil of sin so as to be cured of the love of it, to humble themselves and acknowledge their vileness.

Have you thereupon been brought to an ingenuous confession of sin (Psalm 38:18), with earnest prayers to God for forgiveness when you remember the peculiar aggravations of many of your crimes: how long continued in, against how many helps, warnings, calls, counsels, and obligations to the contrary; how small the temptation, how frequent the repetition, and yet how much willfulness, notwithstanding the various methods of God's grace and providence to reclaim you? Such a conviction cannot long be concealed and hidden. Inquire, therefore, what effects it has had to bring you into the presence of God, there to confess and bewail your folly. "Oh, what a beast, what a fool, what a wretch have I been; thus and thus have I sinned against heaven! How low should I abase myself in the presence of God? How unworthy am I to lift up my eyes to the throne of His glory! How wonderful is His patience, that I am yet alive!"

If you have a serious sense of sin, you will not be able to keep silent; for that is contrary to the confession of sin mentioned in Psalm 32:5: "I acknowledged my sin unto Thee, and mine iniquity have I not hid." While he kept silent, and did not confess his sin, his bones were vexed and his heart was disquieted. But upon a free and full confession to God, His Spirit was calmed and he could look through his penitential tears with hope to God's mercy seat. God requires this confession in order to obtain forgiveness. Jeremiah 3:12–13: " 'Return, O backsliding Israel,' saith the Lord, 'and I will not cause Mine anger to fall upon you, for I am merciful,' saith the Lord, 'only acknowledge thine iniquity.' " And if we confess our sin, the apostle tells us, God is faithful and just to forgive them (1 John 1:9). And the more free and particular we are in our confession of sin to God, so much the better. This cannot be without a holy sorrow and shame in the remembrance of your past folly, your sinfulness and pollution, your ingratitude and rebellion against God, and not merely upon the account of any penal, afflictive consequences by which you have smarted. For godly sorrow will distinguish itself, by the principles and motives of it, to be another thing than merely bowing your head under the burden of affliction. There will be a holy shame and confusion of face in the sense of what you have done, and what you have deserved, so as to tremble at the thought of committing the like sins again; and to fear the temptations that might draw you to it, and make you reckon every burden of affliction tolerable in comparison to the burden of sin. We must consider what we have done, and against whom we have sinned. We must consider what a foolish choice we have made, what grace we have slighted, what mercies we have abused. We must consider how unworthily we have behaved ourselves before God, our Owner, Maker and Sovereign; before Christ, our Savior and Redeemer; and before the Holy Spirit, who has been striving with us: Hereupon we condemn ourselves, and beg that God would not condemn us; we are made sensible of our unworthiness of the least favor and, as the prodigal or publican, beg free mercy, owning His righteousness, if He should deny it. Thus judging ourselves, we justify God and hereby give glory to Him.

This will make His mercy the more welcome, and our prayers the more earnest. Such a sense of sin we must carefully improve to increase our hatred of it. We must have resolutions to forsake it and endeavors against it for the future. This will promote and preserve humility, and a low esteem of ourselves, and entire submission to all the Word and will of God. This will help us to perform every duty, and join in every ordinance, with more meekness and self-abasement; and to bear every affliction as deserving a thousand times worse than we ever yet suffered. This will make us feel more our need of Christ for pardon and sanctifying grace, and make us have daily recourse to Him for the influence of His blood and Spirit: And it will make us ready, upon any just occasion, to confess our sins to men also, if it appears to be for the honor of God that we do so. This will make us more compassionate toward others who have fallen by temptation. This will raise our thankfulness for every little favor, for every beginning of mercy, for everything of grace that we do or may receive from God. And this will cause us readily to embrace and welcome the gospel discovery and revelation of God's forgiveness of sin.

This serious conviction of our guilt and folly will make us own ourselves, the chief of sinners, as knowing the special aggravations of our own sins beyond what we know of others. I do not know, as to other men, their advantages or disadvantages, helps or hindrances by education, knowledge, admonition, counsel, afflictions, and special obligations, as I do my own. I do not know the strength, the urgency, or the importunity of their temptations; whether, if I had the like, I might not have been as bad or worse. I do not know the force and power of bodily constitution, inclining them strongly to some sins. I do not know whether their sins have been committed upon such small temptations as many of mine have been, whether against so many motions of God's Spirit, whether they continued so long without repentance, or against so many helps to repent. I do not know whether there was so much of willfulness and deliberation in other men's sins as I know there have been in my own. I cannot tell but that, regarding other men's faults, there may be something to lessen, to extenuate, to mitigate their guilt, that does not appear. It may be that their principles and intentions were not so bad, and there was more of infirmity, more of mistake and error, more of weakness and surprise in their sins than I know there was in mine. I may hope they did it ignorantly or but seldom, or that the consequence is not so bad, as to God's dishonor and the mischief done to others. I may hope that a great deal of what I hear of their crimes may be false, or that God has given them repentance, though I do not know it. I have reason to consider that they have otherwise many excellent qualifications, many useful and valuable things in them, for which they ought to be esteemed. And so, judging charitably of others, with serious scrutiny into ourselves, we shall see reason to own ourselves as being the chief of sinners. Such a humble sense of our sinful vileness is a part of true repentance, and an evidence of forgiveness.

We cannot suppose this without forsaking sin, to which the promise of pardon is made. If God has forgiven you, He enables you by His Spirit to walk in His ways, to strive, watch, and pray against those sins which with a godly sorrow you have confessed and bewailed, so that you stand in awe of God's authority, and allow yourselves in no willful known sin, or in any negligent omissions of positive, plain duty, but endeavor to walk in all His commandments blamelessly.

However, because of the imperfection of this in the best person, examine what conflicts you have, what opposition you make against sin by renewed, spiritual principles. Is it the desire, care, and endeavor of your souls to have the power of indwelling sin weakened, the habits of grace strengthened, and your obedience more uniform? Are you endeavoring to grow in grace, especially in that grace which is contrary to your particular sin and corruption? Is there an earnest desire, a constant resolution, and and endeavor to bring forth fruits worthy of repentance? The wicked must forsake His way, and the unrighteous man his thoughts, if God abundantly pardons. To forsake it is more than a bare refraining from sin; he must give over all acquaintance with it, and watch continually against it. Whosoever retains any one beloved, darling sin cannot be said to forsake sin, though he refrains from all others. He must forsake it so as to return to God and walk in a contrary path. It must be forsaken as to the affection and love of it, as well as the outward practice. We forsake sin indeed when we loathe it, hate it, and carefully watch against it. A man is said to forsake his meat not when he cannot get it, but when he has no stomach for it; so he forsakes his lusts not when he has no opportunity, but when he has no affection, when there is a habitual enmity in his heart against it, and a constant care in his life to avoid it.

Is there no sin but you are desirous to know and part with? Do you love the holy image of God wherever you discern it? Do you labor after a greater conformity to the divine life? Is it the daily burden of your hearts that you inwardly sanctify God no more, and glorify Him so little in the world? Are your thoughts, desires, opinions, and designs changed? Are the bent of your souls and the course of your lives altered? Can you say, "My heart is inclined to keep Thy statutes always, even to the end. I esteem all His commandments concerning all things to be right, and am desirous to know the whole will of God that I may do it"? And if in particular instances of temptation, you turn out of the way and contract guilt; are you restless and uneasy till you return to God? Can you say with the psalmist, "I have kept the way of the Lord, and have not wickedly departed from Him; for all His judgments were before me, and I did not put away His statutes from me. I was also upright before Him, and kept myself from mine iniquity"? (Psalm 18:21–23).

I confess, as to sins that, by the temperament and constitution of the body, we are more inclined and tempted to than to other sins, a total victory is not to be expected, so as in no degrees to fall into such sins after repentance. Take heed in such cases that you rise again speedily by repentance; that you walk softly and humbly, and that the principal tendency of your repentance and prayer is against those sins—and you will gradually get strength against them so as to say that no iniquity has dominion over you, that you are not the willing servants of sin, so as to love it and deliberately to allow it, but that the desire of your soul is to be freed from it, to have sin subdued as well as forgiven.

What can you say, as to receiving, loving, and prizing Christ, by whom we have forgiveness? Have you heartily accepted Him in all His offices, as offered in the gospel, assenting to His doctrine, as a Teacher sent from God, and our great Prophet? Are you relying on His sacrifice and mediation, as our great High Priest, and being subject to Him as Lord and Ruler? This is receiving Him as Christ Jesus the Lord. This is an honor due to Him for the pardon and salvation He has procured for us. God has made this necessary to our obtaining an interest in the benefits of His death. Do we assent to the doctrine of salvation, revealed and published by Christ, and attested from heaven, as certainly true, that Jesus is the Christ of God, and whosoever believes on Him shall not perish, but have everlasting life? Hereupon are we brought to trust in the mercy of God in Christ, in hopes of His salvation, which is freely offered unto sinners in the gospel? Do we subject ourselves entirely to Him, as one whom God has exalted to be a Prince and Savior, to give repentance and remission of Sins? Are we resolved to be swayed by His authority and ruled by His direction, and to follow Him as our Captain and Commander, Guide and Savior, as long as we live, endeavoring in heart and life to be well pleasing in His sight, so that, whether we live or die, we may be His?

If your sins are forgiven, 'tis for Christ's sake. Consider, what application have you ever made to Him for the cleansing virtue of His blood? Since, if you are washed, if you are pardoned, it must be through the blood of the Lamb, have you looked to Him whom you have pierced, and mourned and been in bitterness for Him, as one who is in bitterness for his firstborn (Zechariah 12:10)? Have you looked upon a crucified Savior, bleeding, groaning, dying for sin, to reconcile us to God and turn us from our iniquities? Have you been answerably affected with the sufferings of Christ, and improved thereby in your hatred of sin?

What thankfulness to God, and what love for Jesus Christ the Redeemer, does the hope of forgiveness excite in you? You read how the penitent in the gospel loved much because much was forgiven (Luke 7:47). How did St. Peter appeal to Christ after the forgiveness of his sin: "Lord, Thou that knowest all things, knowest

that I love Thee." Your love for Christ, and everything
that relates to Him, will be a good argument of the forgiveness of sin, for, having peace with God, the love of
Christ is shed abroad in our hearts. How have your
hearts been affected with thankfulness to God for the
riches of His grace in this forgiveness, for the purchase
of it, for the offer of it, and for any good hope of your
special interest in it? What admiring thoughts have you
of the height and depth, length and breadth of the love
of God in Christ to lost sinners? With what thoughts do
you consider the curse of the law, the terrors of death,
the power of Satan, and the wrath of God (from all
which you are delivered by Christ)? With what affection
do you contemplate the innumerable glorious priv-
ileges, benefits, and blessings that accompany this
forgiveness? With what admiring love to the Redeemer
do you, from time to time, review His condescension
and humiliation; how low He stooped, and how readily;
how great things He suffered, and how willingly, even
to drink the dregs of that bitter cup which but to taste
of would have made men and angels stagger into hell?
With what frame of spirit can you consider Christ offered upon the cross for you, making His soul a ransom
for you? Consider with particular application to yourselves, "He gave Himself for me, shed His precious
blood for me. O my soul, 'twas that I might escape condemnation, that I might be reconciled to God, that my
crimson and scarlet sins might be pardoned, that my
guilty, polluted, miserable soul might be restored to the
image of God, and communion with Him." What affections, what joy have you from such thoughts, especially
at the Lord's Table, when you consider His body broken for you, His blood shed for the remission of your

sins, wounded for your transgressions, bruised for your
iniquities, that by His stripes you might be healed?

Moreover, how are you affected with the sins that
you hope God has pardoned? Do your souls melt with a
godly sorrow for those crimes that you hope are forgiven? What penitent mourning does the psalmist express in Psalm 51, which was penned after God assured
him that his adultery and murder would be forgiven,
and after the prophet had told him, "The Lord hath put
away thy sin!" David wrote, "O Lord, have mercy upon
me, and wash me, and cleanse me, and blot out my
transgression. Against Thee, Thee only have I sinned,
and done this evil in Thy sight."

What influence has God's free mercy in pardoning
sin had upon you, as to shame and sorrow for it? Do the
thoughts that, after all your provocations, God will be
reconciled humble and shame you the more? To this
purpose, the Holy Spirit is promised in the times of the
gospel. Ezekiel 16:63: " 'That thou mayest remember,
and be confounded, and never open thy mouth any
more because of thy shame, when I am pacified toward
thee, for all that thou hast done,' saith the Lord." Is
this the language of your hearts? "He might have condemned me to hell long ago, but through the precious
blood of Jesus I have hopes of forgiveness. Oh, what an
ungrateful wretch have I been! What love have I despised! Against whom have I sinned! How have I rebelled against the God of love and grace, and grieved
His good Spirit! What bowels of mercy have I spurned! I
am astonished at the mercy of God in Christ, offered to
such a rebel as I am. I am confounded at my own vileness, that such heinous iniquities should be blotted
out, that such numberless iniquities should be for-

given; that after I had so often, so long, and so willfully turned my back upon him He should yet call after me, and say, 'I am He, behold, I am He that blotteth out thy transgression for My own name's sake, and will remember thy sins no more.' When God saw me, He might have punished me. He might have made me an example of His justice here, or might have sent me quickly to hell. Or He might have left me unto hardness of heart, to treasure up wrath against the day of wrath. And that He should freely forgive me all, and be graciously reconciled to me, and speak pardon and peace to my soul! Oh, wretch that I have been! Oh, abominable sinner! I abhor myself in dust and ashes."

We find this exemplified in the temper and spirit of those to whom the mercy and grace of God is revealed, especially in the Apostle Paul. He aggravates His sin, and owns himself as the chief of sinners; and never more so than when he is thinking and speaking of Christ's coming into the world to save sinners, and how wonderfully He called him, and showed mercy to Him (1 Timothy 1:14–17). The sight of God's mercy and the sense of His pardon are in themselves proper to raise an admiration of free grace, and to humble the soul before God. It is proper to increase our detestation of sin, and make us loathe ourselves. That which raises our love for God must raise our hatred of sin, and our sorrow for it. Now faith will make us love much, in the sense of having much forgiven.

Besides, the inseperable connection between faith and repentance will evidence this. We shall never adore the love of Christ, as a Redeemer delivering us from the curse, if we are not burdened with the weight of our sins. Nor shall we ever give God the glory of His justice without judging and condemning ourselves by true repentance. Yet the more we see and apprehend of His grace and love in forgiveness, the more broken and contrite, the more humbled, and ashamed, we shall be of our sins against Him.

What can you say regarding the love of your enemies, and forgiving those who have injured and wronged you? There is no better evidence of God's forgiveness of your trespasses than that He has given you a heart to forgive others who have trespassed against you—if it is upon a right principle, because God for Christ's sake has pardoned you, and obliged you to forgive others. "Lord, was there ever such a distance between my brother and me as my sins have made between God and me? Were the injuries I resented from others comparable to the affronts I have offered to God? And has He freely for Christ's sake forgiven me?"

What influence has such a thought to cure and overcome the ruggedness and roughness of your temper and spirit towards others? If God has pardoned you, "go and do likewise" to your brother. "For if you forgive not men their trespasses, your heavenly Father [hath not and] will not forgive you" (Mattthew 6:14). If you have a rancorous, bitter, malicious, revengeful spirit, and will not forgive those who have wronged you, how can you expect forgiveness from God? Do you forgive those who have injured you, as God for Christ's sake has forgiven you? And do you do so heartily, and without dissembling; speedily, and without delay; frequently and often, without limitation, even unto seventy times seven, if our brother offends, that is, as often as he does? And do you do this throughly and without reserve, without exception or equivocation, without remembering past offenses, so as to bear a grudge?

This, I grant, is hard and difficult work; but the Spirit of Christ can enable us to do this. 'Tis the manifest duty of such as are forgiven, and it is a sign and evidence that they are so. Has God forgiven me my scarlet and crimson sins? And shall not I put up with an injury, bear a wrong, endure a reproach or an ill turn, from my fellow creature? Shall I now, in obedience to Christ, forgive him and pass it by?

By these things, if conscience is faithful, you may be assisted to make a judgment whether you have an interest in this forgiveness or not; and, if your sins have been many and great, whether you may, on good grounds, hope, and say that God has abundantly pardoned.

4

Our Confidence in God's Pardoning Sinners

" 'For My thoughts are not your thoughts, neither are your ways My ways,' saith the Lord." Isaiah 55:8

I proceed to the third general point from this passage, the annexed reason from verse 8 why we ought to be fully satisfied and persuaded that God will thus receive returning sinners and abundantly pardon them: because His thoughts are not as ours, nor His ways as ours. And here you may consider,

How this is displayed and expressed, by a double comparison of God's thoughts with ours and His ways with ours.

How it is strongly argued by a most significant similitude: as far as the heavens are above the earth.

The express assurance of the truth of all this from the divine testimony that is added: "Thus saith the Lord." From that phrase no doubt may be made about it.

The whole of this may be comprised in these three particulars:

First, that the thoughts of God, especially in the dispensing of His grace and mercy to returning sinners, are very different from our thoughts, and transcendently above them, as far as the heavens are above the earth.

Second, the ways of God are unlike our ways, and

81

transcendently above them.

Third, God's testimony concerning His thoughts, and ways of grace and mercy to sinners, ought to be credited and depended upon, and is a sufficient ground of faith, "Thus saith the Lord" being added.

It is the first point that I principally design, that the thoughts of God are not as ours, but are very unlike them, and transcendently above them, as far as the heavens are above the earth. This I shall endeavor to prove, confirm, and apply.

Two things will need a little explication: first, how the thoughts of God are different from ours; and, second, how they are transcendently above them, as far as the heavens are above the earth. The first I shall consider more generally, the second with more particular relation to God's pardoning mercy.

1. They are different and not alike. "My thoughts are not as your thoughts." There's an expression to this purpose in Proverbs 19:21 to set out this difference in general: "There are many devices in the heart of man, but the counsel of the Lord shall stand." What is said by Isaiah about God's thoughts is affirmed by the wise man regarding God's purposes: they are not as ours. Ours are vain and uncertain, while His are certain, fixed, and stable.

He makes a threefold difference:

The first difference is in the name. Our thoughts are but devices, God's thoughts are called counsel.

The second difference is that He expresses them in a different number. Our thoughts are in the plural number, with an expression of multiplicity. "There are many devices in the heart of man," but God's purposes are one regular, uniform council.

The third difference is that a different manner of existing is implied. Our purposes are conceived in the heart; we can't bring them forth, nor give them a being out of our own minds. We may contrive and plot, design and resolve, but still the devices are in our own hearts. 'Tis not in our power to accomplish and bring them to pass, to make them firm and fast against opposition. But the counsel of the Lord, and every part of it, shall stand, so great is the difference between God's purposes and ours, between God's thoughts and ours. But that which the text refers to is the dispensing of God's grace and mercy to returning sinners. We must not measure God's thoughts and purposes by our own. The Holy Scriptures represent them to be beyond our fathom, such as cannot enter into our hearts to conceive (1 Corinthians 2:9).

Here I shall show the difference between God's thoughts and ours, as to two remarkable instances among others: first, as to other men's sins and offenses against us, and ours against God; second, as to our afflictions and sufferings from the hand of God. In both respects, our thoughts are very unlike God's, very different from His.

We must not judge God's pardoning mercy to us by our thoughts and carriage towards others who have offended us. He is different from us in these ways:

• We are easily, suddenly, quickly incensed and provoked to anger. Upon every little affront and injury, thoughts of revenge are apt to rise in our hearts. We can bear very little with one another. We must have other thoughts of the patience, forbearance, and longsuffering of God. When the disciples would have called for fire from heaven upon the Samaritans (Luke 9:54), our Lord told them, "Ye know not what spirit ye are of." It is not a divine spirit, it is not the Spirit of God that appears being so easily and presently provoked. Though God is offended and affronted by the wicked every day, and always has the power to execute His vengeance, yet He bears, with much long-suffering and patience, even the "vessels of wrath fitted for destruction." His thoughts are not as ours in this respect: He has revealed Himself to be slow to anger, and of great long-suffering and patience. Let us not conclude that He cannot or will not bear with us because we cannot bear with one another.

• When we are injured and offended by others, we are not easily reconciled; we are not ready to forgive, and we don't seek peace. But the blessed God, whom we despise and provoke by multiplied crimes, waits to be gracious, and invites us to return. He beseeches us to be reconciled. He freely offers to forgive us, and assures us He will abundantly pardon. 'Tis true, the divine Spirit, so far as it is communicated to any, makes them easy to be entreated, forward to forgive, willing to be at peace with those who have injured them, and not to return evil or refuse terms of reconciliation. But ordinarily it is manifest that our temper and carriage to other men is quite different. And we would have very wrong thoughts of God if we apprehend Him to be as unwilling to forgive us as we often are to pardon those who have offended us. Let us think of it with shame, as to those who may have trespassed against us. So what if they began the quarrel, and gave us just occasion of anger; so what if they have been unthankful, and we have obliged them and deserved to be otherwise treated. Shall we yet retain anger, let the sun go down on our wrath, and display an implacable spirit? How different is this from the divine Spirit? And how unlike are our thoughts to God's? You are not to think of God, in this particular, based on what you find in yourselves.

• Our thoughts toward others who have injured us are straitened and limited. We may pardon once or twice, or pass by two or three offenses, but if the same person trespasses again and again several times, we think he has no right to be forgiven, nor are we obliged to pardon him even if he should repent. But our Lord has told us otherwise. If we will be like our heavenly Father, we must not only forgive seven times, but seventy times seven. We have but a little pity; our compassions are limited; we can pardon but a few offenses. But God abundantly pardons and shows mercy to a thousand generations, forgiving ten thousand sins. He has a multitude of mercies (Psalm 5:7), a multitude of lovingkindnesses (Isaiah 63:7). He is rich in mercy and abundant in goodness. He can and does forgive not only sins before repentance, but backslidings afterwards. His compassions do not fail and His mercy endures forever; therefore we are not consumed. You must not measure God by yourselves, nor His thoughts by your thoughts, in this particular.

• If we forgive those who injure us, we are backward to do them good, to treat them with kindness, or to show them favor. It may be that we won't revenge ourselves on them; we'll do them no harm. But we avoid them, are shy toward them, and will not be kind to them. But God's thoughts are not as ours in this respect. He follows us rebels with continued tokens of His favor and loads us with His benefits every day of our lives, though we load Him with our sins. He heaps coals of fire upon our heads. He takes care of us, supports, supplies, and provides for us, and is constantly kind to us, even while we affront Him. And after He has forgiven us, He takes us to be His friends, favorites, and children. All the mercies of your past life, all your present enjoyments, are from Him, against whom you have sinned. You have depended on His providence ever since you had a being, for daily breath and daily bread. He saves you from a thousand deaths and dangers. Your estate, your health, your credit, your liberty, your usefulness, your comfort in relations, and whatever good you have, He gave you. And He has offered to give you His Son, His Spirit, His grace, His glory, and Himself to be your all-sufficient Portion, and your God in covenant—and all this while you have been in rebellion against Him, a wretched criminal against the Lord of your life and the God of your mercies. Oh, how unlike are God's thoughts to ours in this respect, considering what our thoughts are to those who have injured and offended us.

Consider yourselves under affliction and suffering from the hand of God, and see how different God's thoughts and yours are in that respect also. We are wont to conclude that 'tis all from anger and wrath, whereas God says that whom He loves He chastens, that 'tis for our good, and that we are dealt with as sons and not as bastards (Hebrews 12:5–6; Psalm 119:75).

We are petty and froward, peevish and perverse under the rod of affliction, while God's thoughts are thoughts of peace toward us. "When for the iniquity of his covetousness I was wroth," because he had no heart to do good with what I lent him, said God concerning Ephraim, "and I smote him, he went on frowardly in the way of his own heart. Nevertheless I have seen his ways, I will heal him, I will lead him, and restore comfort to him" (Isaiah 57:17–18).

We often under affliction take every hiding of God's face as an utter rejection of us, whereas God has no such thoughts. He still has us in His eye and bears us on His heart. He has our names graven on the palms of His hand and loves us still, though He rebukes us, and will convince us of it by seasonable comforts and deliverance. Jeremiah 31:18, 20: "Is Ephraim my dear son? I have heard him bemoaning himself thus, 'Thou hast chastised me, and I was chastised, as a bullock unaccustomed to the yoke; turn Thou me, and I shall be turned; for Thou art the Lord my God.' " Is he My dear son, or rather is he not so? Is he a pleasant child, is he not so still to Me? "For since I spake against him, I do remember him still; therefore my bowels are turned for him, I will surely have mercy upon him, saith the Lord."

God's thoughts are not as ours, in respect of affliction, as to the continuance of the rod. We are often ready to sink, and be dispirited and overwhelmed in a time of darkness, as if it would never be light. We are ready to give up all for lost, and conclude that God is gone forever, and will be merciful no more. We say, "Our bones are dried up; our hope is lost, and we are cut off for our parts" (Ezekiel 37:11). Whereas God's thoughts are otherwise. He'll make those dry bones live, and fetch them out of the grave of affliction. His thoughts are thoughts of peace, to give us a desired end (Jeremiah 29:11). How many have thought and said in their despair that God's mercy was gone forever, concerning whom He has manifested that His thoughts are not as theirs.

God's thoughts are not as ours as to the end and design which He aims at in our affliction. We think He intends not to refine, but to ruin; not to purify, but to destroy. Whereas in faithfulness He afflicts where He knows we need it, to purge away our dross and take away our sin, and to produce the peaceable fruits of righteousness. "By this shall the iniquity of Jacob be purged, and this shall be the fruit of all, to take away sin" (Isaiah 27:9). Do but wait a little, and you'll see how you have been mistaken in your apprehensions of God, and how His thoughts have been unlike yours.

2. Consider in the second place that God's thoughts are not only different from ours, but transcendently above them, as far and as high as the heavens are above the earth.

Let us look at the kind and nature of them. First, His thoughts of grace and kindness are of an unsearchable depth. "Oh, the depth of the riches of the wisdom and the knowledge of God, whose ways [of mercy as well as judgment] are unsearchable, and past our finding out" (Romans 11:33). There is a depth in them beyond the line of men and angels to measure. Psalm 92:5: "O Lord, how great are Thy works, and Thy thoughts are very deep." In the revelation of God's grace and mercy to sinners by the gospel, we read of the deep things of God, such as "eye hath not seen, nor ear heard, neither hath it entered into the heart of man to conceive" (1 Corinthians 2:9). Such depths amaze the very angels to look into (1 Peter 1:12).

Second, God's thoughts of love and mercy are absolute, sovereign, and independent. 'Tis all after the counsel of His own will, and from the mere good pleasure of His will. This is the source and spring of all His mercy and forgiveness.

Third, God's thoughts of mercy are faithful and effectual. All the declarations of His mercy shall be made good; all the promises of grace shall be fulfilled; all the thoughts of His love shall have their effects. "O Lord, I will exalt Thee, for Thy counsels of old are faithfulness and truth" (Isaiah 25:1). "All His ways are mercy and truth. He keepeth covenant and mercy forever" (Psalm 89:28). Though He visits our iniquities with the rod, yet His lovingkindness He will not take from us, nor suffer His faithfulness to fail.

Fourth, therefore it may be added that God's thoughts are unchangeable, but ours are variable. "The Strength of Israel will not lie or repent, for He is not a man that He should lie, nor the son of man, that He should repent" (1 Samuel 15:29). The Mediator of the New Covenant lives forever to make intercession for sinners.

Fifth, His thoughts of mercy are infinitely pure and infinitely righteous. We shall never fully understand the infinite righteousness of God's thoughts and ways till the revelation of the righteous judgment of God. He is righteous in all His counsels and in all His works; all His ways are equal. "Righteous art Thou, O Lord, when I plead with Thee." The psalmist tells us that God will carry on His thoughts of mercy, perfect His grace, and make it thrive and grow, to show that He is upright, and that there's no unrighteousness in Him (Psalm 92:15).

God's thoughts of grace and mercy are transcendently above ours in the way and manner of His dispensing His grace and mercy. The dispensation of His love and grace to sinners is that which passes knowl-

edge, as to the manner of it. And when this love is shed
abroad in the heart, there is a peace resulting from it
which is better felt than expressed. Something may be
conceived and spoken, but there's a great deal which is
above the reach of words, for we have no line to measure it by, no scale in all the world to weigh it in. We
have nothing to compare it unto that does not fall unspeakably short. We have no kindness, no love, no
charity or affection of one creature to another by which
we can set it forth. The nearest and dearest among men
is as much below this as earth is below heaven. The
riches of His grace in Christ to sinners is called "the
unsearchable riches of Christ." How admirable are the
dimensions of divine grace and love mentioned by the
apostle in Ephesians 3:19, where he speaks of the
length, breadth, heighth, and depth of the love of God
in Christ, which passes knowledge.

Its breadth reaches unto Jew and Gentile, circumci-
sion and uncircumcision, barbarian, Scythian, bond
and free, poor and rich. The vilest and worst of sinners
are not exempted. Mercy is extended to all sorts of persons and cases. 'Tis grace and love, wider than all our
necessities and miseries, sins and wants.

The length of it is from everlasting to everlasting. It
reaches to sinners who were at the greatest distance; it
brings those nigh who were afar off, and calls those
home who were wandering and gone off, so as one
might have thought that they should never return.

The depth of that love and grace is unsearchable.
Unless we understood the depth of that misery and
ruin into which we were sunk by our rebellion against
God, and are delivered from by His pardoning mercy;
unless we understood the horror of that hell of wrath

which our sins deserve, and the extremity of those agonies and torments which our Blessed Redeemer under-
went for our deliverance; unless we knew the power of
God's wrath, and the intolerable, endless misery of lost
souls—we cannot fully understand the depth of this
love.

The height of it is also unsearchable. 'Tis as high as
heaven, to which it will bring us. And it is beyond our
reach to understand, unless we knew the infinite
blessedness of the heavenly glory, which it cannot now
enter into our hearts to conceive, as well as the infinite
misery of condemned sinners in the bottomless pit. We
can no more tell the height than the depth of this
grace of God in thus pardoning sinners.

But to help you a little to some more distinct considerations of this, let me name a few things.

• None does or can so freely pardon and forgive as
God does. If we are brought to forgive those who have
wronged us, 'tis commonly on the entreaty and intercession of some friends who have interest in us and
some power over us, and this after great submissions of
the offender. So it is rather from some external motives
and inducements, than from our own kind and generous inclinations. But it is otherwise when we are pardoned by God. Isaiah 43:25: "I am He that blotteth out
thy transgressions; for My own sake, I'll not remember
thy sins any more." Hosea 14:4: "I will heal their backslidings, and love them freely." Nothing of our prayers
and tears, submissions and humiliations, nothing we
can do or suffer, can make the least compensation to
the justice of God for the contempt and dishonor we
have cast on Him by sin. There is nothing but the free
grace of God in Christ to be eyed, to be pleaded, to be

trusted in, and depended on. In this case, there is no difference between such as are forgiven and such as are left under damning guilt, but what is made by the free grace of God.

• None can pardon so continually. He encourages and commands us to beg for daily forgiveness as well as daily bread. He renews His pardoning mercy every day and every hour. We soon come to the end of our pity, and are quickly tried in forgiving injuries against ourselves. But while we live, we shall stand in need of forgiveness from God. And this is our comfort, that, if we sin, we have an Advocate with the Father, who makes continual intercession for us; and so we hope for continual, daily, renewed pardon.

• None does or can pardon so completely and fully. He blots out our transgressions, so as to remember them no more. He casts them behind His back and throws them into the depths of the sea. Many other blessings He bestows, and lends us for a time, and then calls for them again; but the forgiveness of sin is one of those mercies that are irrevocable and without repentance. We may be without the knowledge of an interest in His pardoning mercy; we may lose the sense of it and forfeit the comfort of it; but if we are reconciled to God, united to Christ, and brought under the bond of the everlasting covenant, though He may chasten us as a Father, and visit our iniquities with stripes, He will not disinherit us or cast us out of His family. His covenant favor and kindness shall never depart, nor shall His covenant of peace ever be removed (Isaiah 54:9). This is as the waters of Noah, which shall never return to overflow the earth. Fatherly love may be angry, but will not turn to hatred.

• None does or can pardon so indifferently, without respect of persons—not only lesser sinners who repent, but the vilest; not only of such a nation, but of any nation; not only such as have sinned thus long and unto such a degree, but those who sin beyond all ordinary bounds and measures. Let the wickedness, unrighteousness, vileness, filthiness, and aggravations of sin be what they will, if you return to God by Christ He will abundantly pardon. This should magnify the riches of His grace to some of you who are interested in this forgiveness. "Lord, how is it that my sins are pardoned when others (not greater sinners than I) have died in their sins, and are undone forever? How is it that I am pardoned, and others who have not been so vile shall never be forgiven? How is it that I have been forgiven, and others who were my companions in sin were left to impenitence and hardness of heart? How is it that many of better parts, of more wit, of more learning, of larger capacities, and who are better accomplished for usefulness and service, are left to go on in sin to their own destruction? How is it that Thy grace has opened my eyes, softened my heart, and made me sensible of sin, and so to value a Redeemer, to seek Him, receive Him, and accept Him?"

• None does or can pardon with such tenderness and compassion. All the affections of parents are stone and adamant compared to His. We read of His delighting in mercy, and of His tender mercies, and lovingkindnesses, of His rejoicing over us to do us good with His whole heart and soul (Jeremiah 32:41). Goodness and love is His very nature, for God is love. He pities us more than the most tender parent ever did a miserable child. "Who is a God like unto Thee, that pardoneth iniquity, transgression, and sin, and passeth by the transgression of His remnant, because He delighteth in mercy?" (Micah 7:18).

Application

All the application I shall make of this shall be to endeavor to bring it home to the case of particular persons in answer to some objections.

OBJECTION 1. Some may be ready to say, notwithstanding all this, "I have such a sight of my own past crimes and their aggravations that none can judge my case like I can, or know the worst of it, like I do. I knew the will of God, and yet disobeyed Him. I have sinned when I knew God forbad it, and threatened with eternal death what I was doing. I have hearkened to temptation, though I had vowed, promised, resolved, and engaged against that very sin I was tempted to. And, which was worse, I had some thoughts of God's seeing me, some apprehensions that He would judge me for it, and yet I went on and sinned. Surely God will never forgive me. If any of my fellow creatures had willfully, deliberately, ungratefully, frequently, and perfidiously despised and affronted, injured and offended me, I, who am but a worm, could have no patience with such a one. Much more may the blessed God resent, remember, and punish such vile iniquities as I have been guilty of."

ANSWER. Consider how high the heavens are above the earth, and, which is more, the difference between the creature and the Creator. His thoughts are not as our misgiving, despairing thoughts. He does and will pardon like Himself, like a God, not after the measures of a finite, passionate, weak man. All that you have said or can say shall be no impediment, if you return to God and seek Him in Christ for forgiveness. He will abundantly pardon beyond what you are able to think or suppose in the like case. God complains of Israel as being prone and inclined to backslide, yet he cannot find it in His heart to destroy them, but expresses a kind of conflict between justice and mercy, and at last resolves, "I am God and not man; therefore I will not execute the fierceness of Mine anger (Micah 11:9), but I will cause them to walk after the Lord" (Hosea 11:10).

He does all things like Himself. If He builds, He makes a world. If He is angry with the world, He sends a flood over the face of all the earth. If He goes out with the armies of His people, He makes the sun stand still, the stars to fight, and the seas to swallow up the most dreadful armadas. If He loves, the precious heart's blood of His beloved Son is not too dear. If any become His friend and favorite through the mediation of Christ, He will make him a king, give him a paradise, and set a crown of eternal glory on his head. Let us not consider so much what is fitting or likely for us to receive, as for so great a God to give and bestow. If we are contrite, humble, penitent, and fly to Jesus Christ as our Refuge of hope, He will think all the meritorious sufferings of His Son, all the promises in His book, all the comforts of His Holy Spirit, and all the pleasures and blessedness of His kingdom little enough for us.

OBJECTION 2. But some will say further, "I once hoped that God had given me true repentance and unfeigned faith, and that I was hearty and sincere in my covenant with God. I had some good hopes that I was reconciled and accepted. I sealed my covenant, set my name to it, and renewed it also at the Lord's Table. And

I thank God, I had some quickening and comfort as I thought, but, wretch that I am, I have revolted since. I have burst those bonds asunder. I have gone back with such abominable backslidings that I can't think that God will ever pardon me who, after I have known the way of righteousness, has turned from the holy commandment. After having been washed, I have returned with the dog to his vomit, and the swine to her wallowing in the mire. I fear I am among those who draw back to perdition, of whom God may say that His soul shall have no pleasure in them."

ANSWER. Consider that God's thoughts are not as yours with regard to returning backsliders. He calls you to return. "O Israel, thou hast fallen by thine iniquity; return unto the Lord thy God." He tells you that His grace and mercy can outdo all that you can think. If you never heard of any who have sinned as you have, or with such aggravated backslidings, He may yet forgive you. "Though your sins be as scarlet, they shall be white as snow; though red like crimson, they shall be as wool" (Isaiah 1:18). If He gives you grace to repent and return, He will forgive. Sins after baptism, sins after unworthily receiving the Lord's Supper, may all be pardoned. There is a fountain opened; there is a ransom found; there is a propitiation made; and there is an Advocate with the Father. You must forgive an offending brother if he repent, even unto seventy times seven. And will not God forgive returning backsliders, and multiply forgivenesses? Our text is the most proper Scripture that can be for such to consider; so that they may not think that no mercy shall be extended to them. They are invited to return, with a promise that God will heal their backslidings (Hosea 14:4). Jeremiah 3:12: "Go and proclaim these words, saying, 'Return, ye backsliding Israel,' saith the Lord, 'and I will not cause My anger to fall upon you; for I am merciful,' saith the Lord, 'and will not keep anger forever." You ought therefore, to add the following words: "Behold, we come unto Thee, for Thou art the Lord our God." Return to Him with all your hearts, and He will receive you graciously and love you freely. The prodigal is entertained upon his return more than the firstborn, as soon as he repents, and says, "I am unworthy to be called thy son." He will heal your backslidings and take away all iniquity: the guilt, the stain, the power, the punishment, and the anguish of conscience. He will not impute your sin. He will purge your conscience from dead works, and enable you to serve and obey Him. The Sun of Righteousness shall arise on you with healing in His wings. The influence of His Holy Spirit shall, by grace and comfort, be restored to you—and all this from His free love and mercy. Nothing is too hard for divine love.

It is, I confess, a real difficulty when one is made sensible of great sins after repentance, and I know of no relief like that which is offered from this Scripture. "I am unworthy," may such a soul say, "but the Lord is gracious. I have misimproved His mercy, and abused His goodness and His patience. What shall relieve me in this case?"

Why, His infinite love, condescension, and grace.

"Well, but I have revolted and gone back, by many aggravated backslidings that stare me in the face."

Yet God is unchangeable. He's not only merciful, but faithful to His covenant. And His faithfulness was never engaged to the angels that fell.

But here's the great objection that will be made to

all this: "This is true, but I am unfaithful; and the un-faithfulness of one party in all covenants disobliges the other party."

In answer to this, I say that He is God and not man. His thoughts are not as ours. With men, in all covenants this is true; but God's thoughts and ways are above ours. Therefore, if I yet return and take hold of His covenant, I may argue that I am within the bond of it, and He will not utterly cast me off, but will forgive me upon repentance. I have read of one in despair whom the devil persuaded that it was in vain to pray to God or serve Him, for he must perish. He would be damned and go to hell when he died. Yet this one went to prayer and begged God that, if he must go to hell when he died, it would please Him to let him serve Him while he lived. Upon this his terrors vanished, being clearly convinced that none could pray that prayer or make such a request who was guilty of the unpardon-able sin, or had sinned the sin against the Holy Ghost.

OBJECTION 3. Some may say further, "But I have had many fears, and some hopes for a time. I thought I was in favor with God, and had an interest in this for-giveness. But I have often heard it, and I believe it, that God never pardons sin where He does not subdue it. Justification and sanctification go together. If the guilt of sin is forgiven, the power of it is broken. But I find corruption is strong; evil inclinations are still stirring and raging. I never imagined that there was such a hell of wickedness in my heart as I now find. There's so much impurity, carnality, pride, and worldliness yet remaining in my soul that I can't think my sins are forgiven, and that God will abundantly pardon me, or has done it, because sin is not mortified and subdued."

ANSWER. God's thoughts and yours are very different in this matter. For He attains wise and holy ends by allowing us to feel corruption, and obliging us to continual conflicts with it; by sanctifying us gradually, and not all at once; by letting us see and feel more of corruption stirring and striving after conversion than ever we knew before. Hereby He engages us in constant warfare all our days, and makes it needful that we may apply to Christ continually as the great Physician of souls. And I beseech you, remember and believe this, that no sin, no corruption that is your burden, that you would rather be rid of than keep, shall ever be damning to you. It may be a sign of more grace that you sensibly complain of corruption more than formerly. If you faithfully oppose it, 'tis an evidence that your hearts are softer, conscience more tender, and that you understand the holy law of God better.

OBJECTION 4. But after all this some will say, "All this is good news to some, but not to me. I have nothing of the spirit of life and power that accompanies forgiveness. I am dead in all my duties. I can't pray. I have no such liberty, freedom, and liveliness in prayer as others have. I come to the Lord's Table, but I have no such sealing, no such comfort, no such assurance, no such joy, no such foretastes of heaven as I believe others have. I keep on in a round of duty, but 'tis not with me as with the living members of Christ. Therefore I can't apply all this to myself with comfort."

ANSWER. God's thoughts are not as yours in this matter. You object that you can't pray with such life and enlargement as others, and as formerly; but is it not your burden? Are you not dissatisfied with yourselves about it? Do you not beg for the spirit of prayer, and to have this ill frame cured? Do you not look up to heaven with daily sighs and groans, and beg for relief from Christ? Are you not weary and heavy laden under this indisposition?

Let conscience be faithful. Is there some great guilt lately contracted? Is there some sin you have not repented of, whereby you have grieved the Holy Spirit of Christ, and this stops your mouths in prayer and shames your faces? Have you rested too much in the outward performance of duty, and attendance on the ordinances of the gospel? You come to the table of the Lord, and look upon it, it may be, as a charm (as too many make it on their death bed); you expect that it shall work like medicine in a natural way, not in a moral one. And by merely coming (whatever you have been or done before, or however negligent you have been in your preparatory work), you expect that it should be all one with you. If you can charge yourselves with any of these things, you must renew your repentance.

If conscience does not accuse you in this matter, consider that God's thoughts are not as yours. He knows what is from the weakness of the flesh and what is from the willfulness of the Spirit. He knows what deadness and distraction may arise from the infirmity of the body, and what is the sin of the soul.

If upon all these accounts you lose the evidence of your acceptance with God, and fear the worst, yet, when a man has lost his acquittal for a debt paid, 'tis a comfort to him to consider that the man he deals with is a merciful, good man, though he cannot find his discharge. God is infinitely gracious, and is ready to restore what you complain you have lost. Such was David's case in Psalm 51. Yea, if you fear that your grace was never true, your heart never right with God, your state never good, there is mercy enough in God to pardon all your former hypocrisy if now you return and seek Him with your whole heart. There are promises of grace in such a case to be pleaded, that God will give a heart of flesh, give a spirit of mourning, put His fear within you, and cause you to walk in His statutes. Therefore, do not fruitlessly bemoan yourself and sit down in despondence, but consult the Word of God, and seek the throne of grace with hope, whatever your objections and temptations are. Whatever you do, take heed of dishonorable thoughts of the grace and mercy of God, and of the security He has given to perform every word of promise wherein He has commanded us to hope.

We are near the end of this year, and many of you design and hope to renew your covenant the next Lord's day at His table. I beg you to consider, and remember for your encouragement, that God's thoughts are not as yours. Whatever sins you have been guilty of this last year, whatever you can charge yourselves with, as to unworthily receiving the Lord's Supper for the time past, yet if now you will seriously examine yourselves, humble your souls, return to the Lord, apply to Christ, and stir yourselves up to be disposed as penitent believers, to renew your covenant vows and engagement to be the Lord's this next time, He will forgive the sins of all your former sacraments; all the sins of the last year and of your past lives, and will seal to you the forgiveness of all sin through the blood of Jesus. You need not, you ought not, to doubt it, for as high as the heavens are above the earth, so are God's thoughts of mercy above ours, and His ways above ours.

5

God's Thoughts and Ways Are
Above Ours in Other Respects

" 'For My thoughts are not your thoughts, neither are your ways My ways,' saith the Lord. 'For as the heavens are higher than the earth, so are My ways higher than your ways, and My thoughts than your thoughts.' "

Isaiah 55:8–9

The disparity between the thoughts and ways of God, and ours here mentiond has special reference to the dispensation of His grace and mercy in pardoning the worst of sinners, who forsake their evil ways and return to God by unfeigned repentance. But in this discourse, I design to consider these words in a larger and more general sense, and to show that the ways of God are not as ours, but as far above them as heaven is above the earth.

By the ways of God we may either understand, first, those He would direct us to walk in: what He would have us to believe and do; or, second, His ways and works toward us in the conduct and management of things by His providence.

In the first sense we read of the way of truth, the way of His commandments, and of walking in the way of the Lord—that is, receiving as true the doctrines He has revealed, and observing the orders and obeying the commands which He has given us.

In the latter sense, by the ways of God I mean His works of providence according to His Word. In both of these—in the declarations of His Word as to what we are to believe and do, and in the works of His providence, what He does with us—there are many things far above us. His ways are not as ours regarding either.

Both of these may very well be comprehended here: the revelations of the will of God by His Word as to faith, worship, and practice, and also His providences and dealings with the children of men according to Scripture revelation. Our ways are not as His as to either. There is a vast disparity between them. In this sense, His ways are very unlike ours, and are transcendently above them, both as to matters of revelation and providence.

POINT 1. God's ways not like ours, but are vastly different.

They are different as to their nature. All His ways and works are perfect, done with infinite wisdom and judgment. And therefore, when Moses published the name of God, he began with this: "He is a Rock. His work is perfect; all His ways are judgment" (Deuteronomy 32:4). They are the fruit of infinite, unerring counsel. But what weakness and imperfection, what defect and folly do we discover in our ways? All His ways are righteous and holy. Psalm 145:17: "The Lord is holy in all His ways, and righteous in all His works." But what impurity and obliquity is there in ours? All His ways are just and equal. He challenges all the world to prove the contrary in any one particular. What does He require of us but what, in the strictest justice, is due? Whereas, how unequal is our carriage towards Him and one another? There is an admirable harmony and agreement in the ways of God, as to all the parts of them, connected one with another. His Word is constant and abiding, steady and consistent, not yea and nay (2 Corinthians 1:19–20). All His promises are yea and amen. The Strength of Israel is not a man that He should lie, nor the son of man that He should repent. But we are mutable, and often cross and contradict ourselves in our ways. The best of men manifest this inconstancy in principle and practice.

There is a further difference between the ways of God and ours in the methods and means used and taken, and the manner of His proceeding to effect an end. His way is to make weak things confound the mighty, and things base and despised, and which are not, to bring to nought things that are (1 Corinthians 1:27–28). We cannot do so. God would not use the wisdom and power of the world for the spreading of the gospel; but by the foolishness of preaching it pleased God to bring men to believe, and make the doctrine of the cross of Christ the power of God to their eternal salvation. The instrument He employed and the methods He used to give success to the gospel plainly evidence this.

This example may serve instead of many others. Was it not an unlikely attempt for a few lowly and obscure persons, such as publicans, fishermen, and tentmakers, without the improvements of education, or the advantages of learning, eloquence, experience and conversation in the world, without the assistance of civil power and authority, or any considerable interest and reputation, to require all mankind to believe in one Jesus, whom they own was crucified, that He was alive, and was Lord and King, and must be received and obeyed as the Christ of God; to tell all the world that all the established rights and religions of their various countries must be laid aside, their wicked customs and courses forsaken, and this new religion of Jesus be embraced that requires the belief and practice of so many things they must account very hard, considering the prejudices and lusts of men? Could they hope that kingdoms and empires, schools and universities, would easily submit to this change; that they should be too hard for the devil, and all the powers of darkness, by preaching the doctrine of a crucified Savior?

And yet, in the space of about thirty years, this new doctrine and religion was not only diffused throughout the greatest part of the Roman Empire, but had reached as far as Parthia and India, even before the destruction of Jerusalem, as our Lord foretold. Matthew 24:14: "This gospel of the kingdom shall be preached in all the world, for a witness unto all nations, and then shall the end come." This success was represented by an angel flying through the midst of heaven, and preaching the everlasting gospel to every nation, kindred, tongue, and people (Revelation 14:6).

This was done without force of arms, and against all opposition imaginable. Their message was entertained, their doctrine credited, and Christ believed on in the world. Many thousands were converted presently, and many more afterward, though the messengers employed could not be sure of success any further than certain of the truth of their doctrine, and of the divine presence and power to accompany them. But they might be almost sure of enduring torments, and losing their lives for publishing such a doctrine, and persisting in it in the manner they did. But the wisdom and the power of God are glorified in succeeding such weak instruments to such excellent purposes.

In all the methods of His providence we find that by weak things He confounds the mighty, and by foolish things (as the world accounts them) He confounds the wise. There are instances of it in the history of Moses, as to the plagues of Egypt. But it was more manifest in the whole frame of Christianity, and in the success and prevalency of it. He defeated the devil's design, and overturned his empire by such means as could never be supposed by reason to do it. By the seed of the woman, whom he had seduced, by the Son of God in our flesh suffering and dying for us, He wrested the victory out of Satan's hands by humbling Himself to the death of the cross, and so, by dying, destroyed him who had the power of death.

There are other instances that might be given where God strengthens the spoiled against the strong, where He brings down those who dwell on high, or where He lays the lofty city low. He layeth it low even to the ground, he bringeth it even to the dust. "The foot shall tread it down, even the feet of the poor, and the steps of the needy" (Isaiah 26:6). The stone cut out of the mountain without hands shall dash in pieces great mountains, all the four great monarchies of the world, and fill the whole earth.

His ways are not as ours in that He often prefers the younger before the elder, and gives them the precedence and principal blessing. Abel was preferred before Cain, and his offering accepted. Abraham, the younger, was chosen to be God's favorite before his older brethren. Jacob was chosen before Esau, and He preferred Ephraim before Manasseh, the elder son of Joseph. So it is observed by the Spirit of God of Noah's children. Shem is preferred, and called the brother of Japheth the elder (Genesis 10:21). And David, the youngest son of Jesse, is chosen to be king, and the man after God's own heart to manifest the freedom of His counsels, and the sovereignty of His grace and providence. "Was not Esau Jacob's brother, yet Jacob have I loved?"

His ways and ours differ also in that He is never frustrated or disappointed in His work, as to what He designs. "He brings the counsels of men to nought, and the devices of the people to none effect, but the counsel of the Lord shall stand" (Psalm 33:10, 11). He speaks the word, and it shall stand. "He confirmeth the word of His servants, and performs the counsel of His messengers, saying to Jerusalem, 'Be thou inhabited,' and to the cities of Judah, 'Ye shall be built'; that saith to the deep, 'Be dry, and I will dry up thy rivers.' He saith of Cyrus, 'He is My shepherd, and shall perform all my pleasure,' even saying to Jerusalem, 'Thou shalt be built,' and to the temple, 'Thy foundation shall be laid' " (Isaiah 44:26–28). Our ways are not like His. He will always overcome when He judges. He will fulfill all His pleasure, and accomplish all that is in His heart, which we cannot pretend to do.

POINT 2. God's ways not only differ from ours, but transcendently exceed them, and are infinitely above them, as high as the heavens are above the earth. There is an unsearchable depth in the ways of God which we are called to adore, but cannot comprehend. We may cry out with the apostle, "Oh, the depth, both of the wisdom and knowledge of God! How unsearchable are His judgments, and His ways past finding out!" (Romans 11:33). "His judgments are a great depth" (Psalm 36:6). "He is wonderful in counsel, and excellent in working. His wisdom is unsearchable, and His ways past finding out" (Job 9:10).

There are many things in divine revelation and providence that transcend our reach. If we will not allow this, but must have a particular reason for all that God speaks and does before we will believe it, what is this but to make His wisdom finite like ours, or ours infinite like His! On this account, the great masters of philosophy in former ages were the worst enemies to the gospel of Christ because the apostles nakedly represented their doctrines without that wisdom, or demonstration from natural principles, which they used, and therefore the gospel was foolishness to them.

Not owning God's ways to be above ours, but making our reason the supreme judge concerning doctrines supernaturally revealed, is the spring of the many errors and blasphemies that abound among us at this day. We may as well measure the justice or injustice of the providential works of God by our will and choice. What He does is just and good, or not, because it is what we like or do not like, as if our finite minds could comprehend whether that can be true which divine revelation has delivered as a true doctrine. We can no more conceive the wisdom and goodness of God in some events of providence than His veracity in some truths revealed.

More particularly, as to Scripture revelation, what we are to believe, let's consider that God's ways and thoughts are above ours: And what is therein asserted, we must receive and credit upon the authority of a divine testimony, though the doctrine there laid down may be such as has no foundation in nature—that is, it could not be known but by divine revelation. 'Tis a sufficient reason for us to believe the doctrine because we find it in Holy Scripture; and we have reason to acquiesce therein because the revelation that is contained in this book we have ground to believe is from God, and so is infallibly true. If we will own our baptism, and take Christ for our teacher, we must receive the truth of what He has revealed upon a divine testimony, even if we can't comprehend how such a Christian doctrine may be reconciled to our common notions of things in other cases.

I grant, the doctrine of the Holy Trinity, for instance, carries a very great difficulty in it, and is more opposed, as being incredible and unintelligible, than other principles of the Christian religion. But this is revealed from heaven, as we affirm and make an article of our faith, if we find it contained in the Holy Scriptures. God's ways being so far above ours will do much to answer the objection of its being incomprehensible.

If God is incomprehensible, why should anything He is pleased to say seem incredible to us? Where He has interposed by His definitive sentence, our reason must submit, and has no right to debate the matter, but ought to approve what God speaks, and subscribe to whatever He writes. The testimony of God, whatever exceptions our reason can make, should convince our judgment, and obliges our faith. Is not His veracity a firm and sure foundation for us to rely upon, without the concurrent testimony of reason? Shall we not believe infinite wisdom and truth upon His own word, unless what He says is in itself credible, and so may be believed, without His testimony? The more we consider what God is, the more easily shall we be persuaded that He is equally to be believed when he affirms what we cannot understand to be true as when He declares that which, by the common principles of our reason, we know is so. If we own a divine revelation, we can no more doubt the one than the other, unless a divine testimony must receive its force from the evidence of our reason. But this would be to destroy all the testimony of divine revelation in supernatural truths, where the evidence of reason fails. So what if we cannot give an account how it is or can be so as we find it in the Scripture; is anything that God says the less credible upon that account? 'Tis the highest reason to believe everything that God has said. His authority has strength sufficient to secure my faith against all such objections as arise only from ignorance, and want of principles to judge by, or from the incomprehensibleness of the object.

It seems plainly to be the design of the apostle in 1 Corinthians 2 to obviate the great objection that is now brought by infidels and Socinians by granting it to be true that what we are taught to believe by the gospel is inconceivable and above the reach of human reason; that many doctrines of the gospel are such as could neither be discovered, nor, when they were, could be received and applauded by the rational part of mankind. It was not the wisdom of men, nor of this world, but the wisdom of God (verses 5–6). The apostle did not go about to persuade the world of the truth of them in such a manner as the wise men among the Gentiles made use of to persuade the people of their opinions. But the gospel, being a divine revelation, they endeavored to prove the truth of it by the demonstration of the Spirit and of power, that is, by supernatural proofs from ancient prophesies, by uncontested miracles, and such like testimonies of God's owning the gospel to be a revelation from Him. So their faith did not stand in the wisdom of men, but in the power of God. And therefore we should not stumble, nor think it strange, if matters of divine revelation should be inconceivable by mere reason.

He lets them know that even this was foretold by the prophets (verse 9), "for it is written, eye hath not seen, nor ear heard, nor hath it entered into the heart of man. . . ." But God has revealed them to us by His Spirit, by which Spirit Christ and His apostles made known this doctrine. And it follows, "The Spirit searcheth all things; even the deep things of God." And therefore, though the things are such as we never thought of before, and we cannot well conceive when they are told us, yet that is no such wonder; for the nature of our own souls cannot be conceived by any inferior being, nor our secret thoughts known by any other of our fellow creatures. Verse 11: "For what man knoweth the things of a man but the spirit of man within him; and so the things of God knoweth no man, but the Spirit of God." As we cannot know the secret purposes of other men till they themselves reveal them, so the counsels of God concerning our salvation, which depend merely upon His own will, none can know but the Spirit of God, and by some revelation from that Spirit, and not by natural reason. "For the Spirit searcheth all things, yea, the deep things of God," that is, the Spirit is acquainted with all His secret counsels.

The great question therefore is whether the revelation that contains such and such incredible doctrines is divine. So accordingly the apostle adds in the next verse that he built his faith not upon the philosophy or inventions of men, but upon the revelation which God has made. "We have not received the spirit of the world, but the Spirit which is of God, that ye may know the things that are freely given us of God." These things could never else have been known, and therefore it should not offend any that we do not endeavor to prove these doctrines by philosophical arguments, but by such as are proper to prove them by, from divine revelation. "Which things also we speak, not in the words which man's wisdom teacheth, but which the Holy Ghost teacheth, comparing spiritual things with spiritual": that is, the revelations of the Old Testament with those of the New. And after all, he tells us in verse 14 that the natural man (who will believe nothing but according to his own preconceived notions from natural reason) "receiveth not the things of the Spirit of God; they are foolishness to him." He will not allow that to be divinely revealed which is above mere natural reason. He considers only the difficulty in the doctrine itself, how it can be true, not what reason he has to believe such a revelation to be from God. And so he cannot know them because they are to be spiritually discerned, that is, to be judged by the revelation and testimony of the Holy Spirit and not by the mere light of reason. They are to be received upon the account of a divine revelation.

The whole tenor of the apostle's discourse seems to obviate or answer this objection of the doctrines of the gospel being incredible and unintelligible. And if we apply it to the doctrine of the Trinity and the incarnation of Christ, it will hold good, notwithstanding the difficulty how three can be one, or how our blessed Savior can be God and man; how there is one divine nature or essence common unto three persons, united in essential attributes, and yet distinguished from each other in order and manner of subsistence, and by peculiar idioms and relations. These notions may puzzle our reason to conceive, but should not stagger our faith to believe, as revealed in Holy Scripture.

Considering what God is, and what we are, 'tis unreasonable to reject any article of faith because we cannot fully conceive the nature and manner of its being true. Shall we compare our darkness with His incomprehensible light, or equal our understanding with His? Shall we refuse to believe what He has declared for truth unless we can reconcile it with our maxims? What room is there left for faith at this rate? What credit is given to divine testimony if we believe nothing to be true in God's Word unless we can fathom it, and would otherwise believe without His testimony?

If we consider the imperfections of our understandings, both as to the finite nature of the soul, and the manifold experience we have of it every day, we must be content to be ignorant of many things. What is well known in many civilized countries may appear very strange to a great part of the heathen world. The fabric of a watch; or the mutual communication of thoughts by writing, would perhaps be as unconceivable to an Indian as the mystery of the Trinity is to us; yet the truth of the thing does not depend upon his conception of it.

And how short do the wisest and most knowing men come of the infinite knowledge of God? Though we are certain of the truth of His being, how little do we know of His nature and perfections? How far above our apprehensions is the eternity? All successions of time are ever present to Him and subject to His view. His self-existence, His immensity, His omnipresence, and His prescience of the most contingent events—how far above us they are!

And since we do not have a perfect knowledge of the subject, we must hearken to what God Himself says of His own nature, who knows it best. And we ought in reason to inquire whether the doctrine of the Holy Trinity is contained in that revelation which we receive, and can prove to be divine; if we find it there, let the doctrine be never so incredible and unintelligible, God is so far above us, and His ways and thoughts above ours, that we ought not to reject it upon that account. As the heavens are higher than the earth, His wisdom is as the heavens, the highest and top of all wisdom. Man's is as the earth, beneath which there is no degree but that of hell and darkness, so that the things are too great and sublime for us to determine about.

Were this duly considered, we would find that we cannot have so much evidence of a doctrine's being false because it is unconceivable as there is evidence of its being true by being contained in Scripture revelation. As to the truth of things concerning finite nature, we may judge by our reason; but where the object is infinite, it is no argument against the truth of a thing that we cannot comprehend it, unless a contradiction is proven, which there is none here.

It has often been proved that God might justly require of us in general the belief of something we cannot comprehend, and that they who reject the mysteries of Christianity run into greater difficulties than those who assert them. What is incomprehensible as to the manner may be a necessary article of faith, as far as it is revealed. We don't assert three gods, only one. Three persons and yet but one person would be contradictory; but the Scripture says that these three (Father, Word, and Spirit) are one God. And we ought to distinguish between numbers, and the natures of things. For three to be one is a contradiction in numbers; but whether an infinite nature can communicate itself to three different subsistances, without such a division as is among created beings, must not be determined by bare number, but by the absolute perfections of the divine nature: This must be owned to be above our comprehension. Therefore, for any to assert that there cannot be a plurality of persons without a plurality of natures, or that there cannot be a communication of nature without an identity of persons, is to pretend to know more of the infinite nature of God than any modest man ought to pretend to.

It is certain the objections from the inconceivableness of this doctrine are not so great as the evidence we have that such a doctrine is contained in the Holy Scriptures, and that this Scripture is of God.

Let me add that to pay adoration and divine worship to Christ (as the Christian Church has done in all ages), and to trust in Him for pardon and eternal life, and yet believe Him to be only a man, destroys all the reasons and arguments of giving divine worship to God only. For to do this, and not own Him to be omnipresent, omniscient, and almighty, to not own Him to be the true and eternal God, is a greater absurdity and contradiction than all that can be objected against the doctrine of the Sacred Trinity. While they pay Him divine honor, they must consider Him as the God whom all the angels worship, and yet at the same time they deny Him to be so: And that because they cannot conceive how Father, Son, and Spirit could be one God. But let us remember what God is and what we are; and how His ways and thoughts are above ours. Let no man therefore deceive himself. "If any man among you seem to be wise in this world, let him be a fool that he may be wise; for the things of God knoweth no man but the Spirit of God, who revealeth them unto us."

God's ways are above ours in the dispensations of His providence: It would be easy to show this in a multitude of particulars: in His sparing and forbearing us, in restraining and preventing us, in keeping and preserving us, and disappointing our enemies, overuling our affairs, directing our conditions, and governing all that befalls us, good or evil, accidental or premeditated, and turning all to wise and gracious purposes beyond our thoughts.

With what perfect wisdom is everything managed in the government of this world? Even the wickedness of men is made to serve the purposes of His glory! How wonderfully has God honored His mercy, power, holiness, justice, and truth in redeeming and saving sinners by Jesus Christ, with greater advantage than if our first parents had continued innocent!

His ways are not as ours, but are above them in governing the minds of men, turning their hearts, influencing their counsels, and changing their thoughts to bring about and fulfill His own. His ways are above ours in making use of very unlikely instruments, weak means, yea, such as in appearance are contrary, to effect

His own purposes in the government of nations, of particular families and persons.

The ways of His providence are above ours, in His disposing crosses and afflictions, temptations and hardships, unto those He loves best, and permitting others to live in peace and quiet.

His ways are not as ours, but are above them, in that the very falls and faults, crimes and follies of good men are overuled for much good and great transgressions before conversion, and are made servicable to excellent purposes afterwards. What was poison in nature becomes medicinal by divine grace. He who stumbles on the way gets ground by it, if it helps him to mend his pace, to walk faster and more warily. How many can say, "If it had not been for such and such falls, I would never have known so much of my own weakness and frailty. I would never have had such temptation, and seen how unable of myself I was to resist it. I would never have had so hearty a detestation of sin, such a tenderness of conscience, such an awe of offending God, so fervent a zeal to please Him, so sweet a sense of His mercy, so thankful an acknowledgment of His grace in delivering and recovering me."

The very remainders of corruption in the hearts of men which they bewail, pray, and strive against shall serve to convince them of their necessary dependence on God's grace. It shall cause them to walk humbly with God; it shall make them more circumspect and watchful against temptation, and raise their esteem and value of the blood of Christ, and His constant intercession in heaven. God hereby assists us to keep conscience tender, excites our diligence after further degrees of mortification, and quickens us to press on, by growth in grace, toward perfection.

Moreover, His ways are above ours in the conversion of sinners, as to the subjects He makes choice of; as to the season and time of their change; and as to the means and methods by which that is accomplished and brought about. The wind blows where it will, and the Holy Spirit (by the ministry, oftentimes, of weaker ministers) works powerfully and savingly in whom He will, "both to will and to do of His own good pleasure." One is awakened, convinced, and pricked to the heart by a sermon. Another, in the same seat, under the same sermon, feels nothing. Some are reached sometimes by a soft, still voice, and at other times by thunder. Sometimes the most unlikely are taken and effectually called, while others are left; and this after many years' delay and discouragement, and no hopeful prospect, but the contrary. Some out of wicked families are converted, and others, after strict and religious education, become and continue most vile and profligate. What different success the gospel has in some places, at some times, and to some persons, and at different times in the same place? Yet it is the same message and the same preacher! Sometimes it has success on the weaker and more ignorant sort, and sometimes on the more learned; sometimes on elder persons, and often on younger ones, who have discovered much of the grace of God betimes, with less advantage of education than others. And at the last hour, some malefactors, under a sentence of death have been truly penitent and are accepted, as well as the thief on the cross—some by their own afflictions, some by the warning of other men's examples, and by other means, as well as by the plain preaching of the Word, the ordinary means.

His ways also are above ours in punishing men in this life; in making some examples who were not greater sinners than others, as our Lord has expressly told us in Luke 13. He would not spare Job's ten children upon the intercession and prayer of their righteous father, though we don't read that they were wicked. Yet He would have spared many thousands who were wicked in Sodom and Gomorrah, and the cities of the plain, if there had been but ten righteous persons among them.

His ways are above ours in bringing good out of the evil of punishment, and using wicked instruments to accomplish other ends and purposes than they designed. The like might be said of God's ways in saving and delivering His people in extraordinary dangers, tarrying till their enemies are at the very height of their wickedness; and when there is least prospect or appearance which way deliverance should come than to interpose by seasonable salvation.

Application

No wonder then if we so often err in our thoughts and conceptions of the ways and works of God if they are as much above ours as heaven is high above the earth; if they are so unsearchable and beyond our reach that we can see but a little part of His ways, and cannot understand the connection and dependence of one part with the other, or the design of the whole. His way is in the whirlwind; the clouds are the dust of His feet, and His footsteps are not known. He hides Himself that we cannot see Him (see Job 33:7–9 and Nahum 1:3).

As to His ways of grace and mercy, I have largely

shown in the foregoing sermons that He is more gracious than we believe. He is able to do, does, and will do
more than we are able to ask or think (Ephesians 3:20).
We think (it may be) that He will never receive us after
such and such transgressions, and yet He does. We
thought He would never pardon us, and yet He has forgiven. We said in our despair that He was gone and
would never return, and yet the light breaks out again,
and we have found it to our comfort.

If His ways are so much above ours, then what reason we have to reverence and adore God in all His ways
and works, believing His wisdom, goodness, and truth.
We glorify God by crediting His Word, trusting His
practice, following His counsel, and submitting to His
providence though the doctrine is very mysterious, the
providence very dark, the duty very difficult, and what is
promised a great way off, and to sense unlikely.

The more we contemplate the wonders of His providence and grace, the higher veneration we shall have
for Him, and abase ourselves before His glorious
majesty. If we speak of strength, He is strong; if of
goodness, He is love; if of wisdom, He is the only wise
God.

It is unreasonable then to object against this providence just because we cannot comprehend the wisdom
and justice of every event. We may object ourselves into
atheism and infidelity if we will not adore His unsearchable wisdom in the government of the world.
"His judgments are a great deep" (Psalm 36:6). 'Tis in
vain for us to pretend to go to the bottom of them,
when He Himself has declared that they are unsearchable. We should rather admire God, and confess our
own ignorance when the great apostle himself declares

that God's ways are past our finding out (Romans 11:33).

We may be certain that all He does is agreeable to infinite wisdom and righteousness. As long as we own Him to be God, we can be sure that He will do nothing repugnant to those perfections.

Besides, He has appointed a day wherein He will satisfy all the world by the revelation of His righteous judgment. In the meantime, He does great things past our finding out, and wonderful things without number (Job 9:10). There are depths and mysteries in divine providence that we must acknowledge to be unsearchable. Let us not then censure what we cannot understand, what we cannot fathom. Is it strange that incomprehensible wisdom should do incomprehensible things? We should not therefore inquire too curiously into the secrets of His providence, nor determine anything rashly concerning it, which is not revealed to us (see Dr. Isaac Barrow's sermon on "The Unsearchableness of God's Judgments," from Romans 11:33, in *The Works of Isaac Barrow,* reprinted by AMS Press).

We are well assured that He made the world; and yet there are many questions about the work of creation that may puzzle the wisest and most diligent inquirer. So in the government of the world, there are many things above our reach, and yet we may be assured an unerring wisdom governs all. We are so ignorant and short sighted, and the designs of God are so far beyond us, and the means He uses are oftentimes so various, and their connection with His design so much concealed from our weak eyes, that no wonder if we are often at a loss—especially when all the particulars of His works of providence that make up the beauty of the whole are wonderfully interwoven together (one passage and one action having a certain reference to a million others, yea, unto all others, from first to last), so that it is not strange if we do not comprehend the reasons of all events, and do not discern the wisdom and righteousness of God, as to many particulars, while we yet believe Him to be wise and holy in all His ways, and righteous in all His works.

Hereafter, when He has finished His whole design, from the beginning to the end (whereof we now see but a small part), the difficulties that perplex and shock us for the present will be all resolved. What is now covered with darkness shall appear in open light, and what is now a riddle will cease to be so; for all the changes and revolutions of the world, public and private, as to nations, families, and persons, will all be found to have been directed in the wisest and best manner; and to have been one complete and orderly means to bring about His wise and holy counsel for His own glory.

Let us therefore adore Him, considering that His ways are above ours, for if we do not now see a reason for the truth of all that God speaks, or the wisdom of all that He does, we may yet be assured that God is true, wise, and good. And we ought to lay our hands on our mouths and acquiesce for this very reason, because His ways are so much above ours.

What reason then have we to put our trust and confidence in God, to believe what He promises, and leave it to Him to fulfill His Word in His own time and way? His ways are so much above ours that when we think Him furthest off, He may be nearest doing that for us which we desire. If God did not choose our condition for us, we would easily be undone by our own choice.

But we may and ought to trust Him who knows what is always, and upon all accounts, best for us. Whereas there is no man of the clearest foresight, and of the greatest wariness, but may easily be deceived and mistaken as to what is good for him in this life. We find this was the result of the wise man's thoughts concerning the affairs of this world. Ecclesiastes 6:11–12: "Seeing there be many things that increase vanity, what is man the better? For who knoweth what is good for man in this life; all the days of his vain life, which he spendeth as a shadow? For who can tell a man what shall be after him under the sun?"

We often desire and choose such a temporal good as is proper to serve and promote some particular interest and design, but cannot tell whether it will be prejudicial to our main and greatest interest. If it would be so, 'tis a kindness to be disappointed. Besides, we are too apt to consider ourselves as single and alone, in a private capacity: God alone knows what is best for us, as we are parts of the whole community, members of the universe, and stand related to other men It may be that what we desire to have, be, and do that which is more for the public good, should be enjoyed by others and done by others. Such a condition of life, such a place of employment, such a station of service, we reckon to be very desirable for us, when perhaps God knows that we shall do more good in another place, and that some other will be more useful, and more a public blessing in that same post. Accordingly, we should leave it to His providence, who appoints us our work, to assign us our station, and opportunity for it.

And here 'tis most certain that our spiritual and eternal good is greatly concerned. It may be that what we wish for, as a desireable, temporal blessing, would be to our prejudice and disadvantage, as to the welfare of our souls. How many, on this account, have seen reason to be thankful for afflictive disappointments, as to many things they endeavored and desired, but God ordered it otherwise for their best good. "No affliction for the present is joyous, but grievous, but afterwards it produceth the peaceable fruits of righteousness" (Hebrews 12:11). Uninterrupted health, peace, plenty, reputation, joy, and comfort in relations, may be denied us in faithfulness and kindness. For God alone knows whether it would not interfere with our spiritual good.

It is an obvious and daily instance as to riches, and the increase of an estate. Many a poor man (or suppose one in a middle condition) fancies that if he had a great estate, what a great deal of good he would do. With his large heart, he would supply the necessities of the poor. How many generous and charitable things he would undertake. He would fain help and relieve the poor (he tells you) if he could, and therefore his desire for riches, and his diligence in seeking them, is but that he may do good. But when this man succeeds, how common is it that his heart and purposes are changed with his condition? His desire for and love of money grows with his estate, so that he is as unable to do the good he desires to do as before. The poor are unrelieved, and he thinks himself as far from an ability to relieve them now as when he had but half of that which now he has. Besides that, he is tempted to forget God in other instances, and falls into luxury and vanity, intemperance and pride; and consequently, it would have been better for him to have continued in a lower station. He is really a loser by his gain of riches, and 'tis well if He is not finally and forever lost.

It is therefore our wisdom, as well as our duty, for us to leave all events to God, whose ways are so far above ours. If we reflect upon our own ignorance, as to what shall be on the morrow, how easily may tomorrows' events unravel our scheme of thoughts, and frustrate the most probable designs that can be laid? And how ignorant are we of what the train of consequences may be upon what we design. Unless we know what will follow upon it, we cannot tell whether it will prove to be a mischief or a blessing. "You thought evil against me," said Joseph to his brethren when they sold him into Egypt, "but God meant it for good, to bring it to pass (as at this day) to save much people alive" (Genesis 50:20).

Many have lamented with impatience that they came too late to such a port, to sail with such a convoy, or to embark on such a ship; and yet within a little while they have blessed God for the disappointment; having heard that the ship was cast away, or taken by an enemy, and all the passengers drowned or made prisoners. Whereas God knows all the consequences of things, having all causes and effects in view, and all the links of the chain in His own hand, and therefore can never be mistaken in what is best. Let us therefore trust Him to dispose of us and ours according to His own good pleasure.

How reprovable then is it to limit and prescribe to God, or to censure Him concerning His ways and works, which are so much above us? He is not bound to give us an account of all His matters, or to utter all His words for the satisfaction of our curious and proud inquiries. We are not to direct Him what to do, as if we would teach Him knowledge, as if He had not done everything for the best in what befalls us or others. "Shall he that contends with the Almighty instruct Him? He that reproveth God, let him answer it" (Job 40:2). With these words Elihu silenced Job (33:12): "Behold, in this thou art not just. I will answer thee. God is greater than man." That is, "His ways are above ours. Let us take heed of censuring His infinite and eternal wisdom. For we are but of yesterday, and know nothing. We cannot search His secret counsels. They are as high as heaven; what can you do? They are deeper than hell; what can you know? His kind designs, or faithful, gracious purposes, may be concealed from us." As our Lord told Peter in John 13:7: "What I do, thou knowest not now; but thou shalt know hereafter."

Labor to submit to God in all His ways without murmuring or repining. 'Tis both our duty and interest to do this from what has been discoursed. The mind of God revealed in His Word, and the will of God declared in providence, must both be submitted to, whatever objections we may have concerning either. As to the latter, we know not what is fittest to desire or choose for ourselves or others. We often ask that which God knows would be hurtful, and are dissatisfied with that which He intends for our good. We would choose that which, it may be, would be injurious to God, to ourselves; and to the world. We often repine at that as a calamity which God intends us as a benefit, and afterwards proves to be so. Let us not then complain of His government or repine at His providence. Let us not presume to demand a reason why such a cross befalls us, or why we are deprived of such a comfort. Let us not dare arraign His wisdom and sovereignty at our bar, but patiently submit to Him and wait for Him, He is a God of judgment, and His thoughts and ways are above ours.

Therefore, take comfort from this consideration. He may and can turn all for good that we deprecate or complain of as evil. He may be bringing about that which we have long prayed for by those very means which have a quite contrary appearance for the present. He has a thousand methods that we can't conceive of to effect His own purposes—and He knows the fittest time.

Whatever difficulties we are under, whatever burdens we feel, whatever temptations we meet with, whatever disappointments we have had or may have, whatever inward or outward distresses we may be exercised with—still remember that God's ways are far above ours. Though He seems to neglect us, or to hide Himself from us; though He seems to shut out our prayers and not to regard our cry, yet He knows what to do, when to do it, and what is the best manner: He has promised that all things shall work for our good, and that He will never leave us nor forsake us. Therefore, resign yourselves to God, resolving entirely to follow Him; though like Abraham, you do not know where He will lead you. Resolve to submit your understandings and wills to him, to believe whatever He declares to be true, to approve whatever He appoints and bear whatsoever He imposes, and to undertake and do all that He requires. Patiently wait on the Lord and keep His ways, who is a God of judgment. You have sufficient encouragement to hope in His mercy, and trust Him to fulfill His Word in His own method, because His ways and thoughts are not as ours.